PARAGON ISSUES IN PHILOSOPHY

D1558741

PARAGON ISSUES IN PHILOSOPHY

Problems in Personal Identity   James Baillie

*Individual, Community, and Justice: Essential Readings in Social and
  Political Philosophy*   Jeffrey Barker and Evan McKenzie, Editors

Philosophy and Feminist Criticism: An Introduction   Eve Browning
  Cole

Philosophy of Science   James H. Fetzer

Foundations of Philosophy of Science: Recent Developments   James H.
  Fetzer, Editor

Philosophy and Cognitive Science   James H. Fetzer

Foundations of Cognitive Science: The Essential Readings
  Jay L. Garfield, Editor

Meaning and Truth: Essential Readings in Modern Semantics
  Jay L. Garfield and Murray Kiteley, Editors

Living the Good Life: An Introduction to Moral Philosophy   Gordon
  Graham

Philosophy of Sport   Drew Hyland

Philosophy of Technology: An Introduction   Don Ihde

Critical Theory and Philosophy   David Ingram

Critical Theory: The Essential Readings   David Ingram and Julia
  Simon-Ingram, Editors

Social and Political Philosophy   William McBride

*Race, Reason, and Order: Philosophy and the Modern Quest for Social
  Order*   Lucius Outlaw

Metaphysics: A Contemporary Introduction   John Post

African Philosophy: The Essential Readings   Tsenay Serequeberhan,
  Editor

Introduction to Modern Semantics   Ken Taylor

Woman and the History of Philosophy   Nancy Tuana

FORTHCOMING TITLES

Heart and Mind: Essays in Feminist Philosophy   Eve Browning Cole and
  Nancy Tuana, Editors

Introduction to the Philosophy of Law   Vincent Wellman

THE PARAGON ISSUES IN PHILOSOPHY SERIES

At colleges and universities, interest in the traditional areas of philosophy remains strong. Many new currents flow within them, too, but some of these—the rise of cognitive science, for example, or feminist philosophy—went largely unnoticed in undergraduate philosophy courses until the end of the 1980s. The Paragon Issues in Philosophy Series responds to both perennial and newly influential concerns by bringing together a team of able philosophers to address the fundamental issues in philosophy today and to outline the state of contemporary discussion about them.

More than twenty volumes are scheduled; they are organized into three major categories. The first covers the standard topics —metaphysics, theory of knowledge, ethics, and political philosophy—stressing innovative developments in those disciplines. The second focuses on more specialized but still vital concerns in the philosophies of science, religion, history, sport, and other areas. The third category explores new work that relates philosophy and fields such as feminist criticism, medicine, economics, technology, and literature.

The level of writing is aimed at undergraduate students who have little previous experience studying philosophy. The books provide brief but accurate introductions that appraise the state of the art in their fields and show how the history of thought about their topics developed. Each volume is complete in itself but also complements others in the series.

Traumatic change characterizes these last years of the twentieth century: all of it involves philosophical issues. The editorial staff at Paragon House has worked with us to develop this series. We hope it will encourage the understanding needed in our times, which are as complicated and problematic as they are promising.

John K. Roth   Frederick Sontag
Claremont McKenna College   Pomona College

PHILOSOPHY OF SCIENCE

ALSO BY JAMES H. FETZER

Author

Scientific Knowledge: Causation, Explanation, and Corroboration
Artificial Intelligence: Its Scope and Limits
Philosophy and Cognitive Science
(Paragon House)

Co-author

Paragon Glossary in Artificial Intelligence/Cognitive Science
(Paragon House)
Paragon Glossary in Epistemology/Philosophy of Science
(Paragon House)

Editor

Foundations of Philosophy of Science: Recent Developments
(Paragon House)
Principles of Philosophical Reasoning
Aspects of Artificial Intelligence
Sociobiology and Epistemology
Epistemology and Cognition
Probability and Causality

Co-editor

Program Verification: Fundamental Issues in Computer Science
Philosophy, Language, and Artificial Intelligence
Philosophy, Mind, and Cognitive Inquiry
Definitions and Definability

JAMES H. FETZER
UNIVERSITY OF MINNESOTA, DULUTH

PHILOSOPHY OF SCIENCE

PARAGON
ISSUES IN
PHILOSOPHY

PARAGON HOUSE · NEW YORK

FIRST EDITION, 1993

PUBLISHED IN THE UNITED STATES BY

PARAGON HOUSE
90 FIFTH AVENUE
NEW YORK, NY 10011

LIBRARY OF CONGRESS CATALOGING-IN-PUBLICATION DATA

FETZER, JAMES H.
    PHILOSOPHY OF SCIENCE / JAMES H. FETZER.—1ST ED.
        P. CM.—(PARAGON ISSUES IN PHILOSOPHY)
    INCLUDES BIBLIOGRAPHICAL REFERENCES (P.   ) AND INDEXES.
    ISBN 1-55778-481-7
    1. SCIENCE—PHILOSOPHY.   I. TITLE.   II. SERIES.
    Q175.F417   1993
    501—DC20   91-47946
                                                        CIP

MANUFACTURED IN THE UNITED STATES OF AMERICA

CONTENTS

Preface   xi
Acknowledgments   xvii

Chapter 1. *What is Science?*   1

The History and Philosophy of Science • The Aim of Science •
The Nature of Explications • The Analysis of Language • The
Analytic and the Synthetic

Chapter 2. *Laws and Lawlikeness*   22

Lawlike vs. Accidental Generalizations • Support for Counterfactuals • The New Riddle of Induction • Universals and Dispositions • Permanent Properties

Chapter 3. *What are Scientific Theories?*   43

The Standard Conception • The Analytic and the Synthetic
(Again) • The Dogma of Reductionism • The Semantic Conception • The Place of Provisoes

Chapter 4. *Explications of Explanation*   63

The Covering-Law Model • The Statistical-Relevance Model •
Long Runs and Single Cases • The Causal-Relevance Model •
Questions about Explanations

Chapter 5. *Probability and Inference*   85

The Symmetry Thesis • Chance and Games of Chance • Determinism and Indeterminism • Frequencies, Propensities, and Personal Probabilities • Probability as a Guide in Life

Chapter 6. *The Problem of Induction*   106

Validation, Vindication, and Exoneration • Rationality, Morality, and Decision • Frequencies and More Frequencies • The Justification of Induction • The Fundamental Question about Chance

Chapter 7. *The Growth of Scientific Knowledge*   127

Conjectures and Refutations • Normal Science vs. Revolutionary Science • The Methodology of Research Programs • Inference to the Best Explanation • Discovery, Inference, and Unification

Chapter 8. *The Nature of Scientific Knowledge*   147

Instrumentalism vs. Realism • Naturalized Epistemology • Evolutionary Epistemology • Paradigms, Change, and Truth • Could Sociology of Science Be(come) Philosophy of Science?

An Overview   169

For Further Reading   175

References   179

Index of Names   185

Index of Subjects   189

PREFACE

This book has been composed with two audiences in mind. First and foremost, it has been written as an introduction to the *central problems* that define the philosophy of science today. In this respect, it is meant to supply a foundation for inquiry into the nature of science, its methods and its products. Second and collaterally, it has been written to propose *promising solutions* to the problems that define the philosophy of science today. In this respect, it should also appeal to a more advanced audience.

The rise of science has been a distinctive feature of human history as it has developed in recent times, especially since the seventeenth and eighteenth centuries. Its influence has been so vast and pervasive that it appears to be virtually impossible to understand the world today without understanding the nature of science. Science and the technologies it makes possible have transformed every area of life from industry and entertainment to transportation, communication, and medicine. It dominates modern life.

The rapid growth of scientific knowledge, however, threatens to overwhelm even the most enthusiastic student. While there was a time when a person might have known everything there was to know that scientists had ever discovered, those times are long past. What we need instead is a *general framework* by means of which we might be able to understand science without knowing all there is to know that science has discovered. We need to know the goals and methods that make something a *science*.

Those who engage in attempts to develop a general framework for understanding the nature of science are philosophers of science, even when they are not called by that name. Scientists who consider the methods of science are likewise engaging in the philosophy of science, even if they do not think of it that way. Not surprisingly, different thinkers have diverse ideas about what makes something science. In this book, we shall consider and evaluate the merits of various notions about what science is about.

An alternative approach with its own appeal might be to make a list of activities that are called "science" by those who pursue them. Unhappily, this does not get us very far, since some activities— Library Science, Mortuary Science, and Military Science—are called "sciences" without being sciences, while other activities— physics, chemistry, and biology—are sciences but are not always called by that name. If matters were that simple, then neither you nor I would need to study the subjects dealt with in this book.

It may be useful to suggest some general features that may be helpful in distinguishing between three disciplines that can easily be mistaken for each other but which are really very different in their methods and goals:

Empirical Science aims at the discovery of general principles by means of which particular events that occur during the history of the world might be explained and predicted, where those principles are accessible to experience and may be tested on the basis of observation and experimentation.

The History of Science attempts to reconstruct the hypotheses and theories that different scientists have advanced and the kinds of observations and experiments that they have conducted in their efforts to discover the general principles by means of which the world itself may be understood.

The Philosophy of Science attempts to reconstruct those principles and procedures by means of which the pursuit of science might be possible as an activity whose methods are suitable to attain its goals, since otherwise the pursuit of science cannot properly be regarded as a rational activity.

Putting the matter in simpler terms, the goal of empirical science is to construct *a model of the world* and the goal of the history of science is to *record past efforts to construct a model of the world*, whereas the goal of the philosophy of science is to construct *a model of science*. The models that scientists construct are usually referred to as "theories," while those that philosophers construct are also called "explications," but they can be appropriately described as models of the world and as models of science.

The section of this book entitled "References" includes the authors and titles of the sources that were of special interest to me in the preparation of this book. If you would like to pursue a topic but do not know where to begin, take a look and see if something relevant is listed there. The section entitled "For Further Reading" provides a sketch of other works that deal with the subjects discussed in corresponding chapters. Many of them discuss alternative solutions to the central problems within the philosophy of science.

TO
CARL G. HEMPEL
AND
WESLEY C. SALMON

ACKNOWLEDGMENTS

The cover is a comparative chart of the world from the Ptolemaic to the Copernican. It previously appeared in S. K. Heninger, Jr., *The Cosmological Glass: Renaissance Diagrams of the Universe* (San Marino, CA: The Huntington Library, 1977), p. 71. The author gratefully acknowledges its use here by permission of The Henry E. Huntington Memorial Library.

It has been my good fortune to have studied with some of the leading figures in the philosophy of science during some of their most productive periods. I received my A.B. in 1962 with a thesis on explanation for Carl G. Hempel and my Ph.D. in 1970 with a dissertation on probability and explanation for Wesley C. Salmon. Their influence—and that of Karl R. Popper—upon my intellectual development, as will be evident, has been profound.

The following pages are intended for use as an independent text or in collaboration with my edited work, *Foundations of Philosophy of Science: Recent Developments* (Paragon), which I tried out with my students in Philosophy of Science Spring Term 1991. Their responses contributed to both projects. Among many others whose comments and criticism have influenced me, I would especially like to thank Robert Almeder, Wayne Davis, Ellery Eells, Linda Sartorelli, and the anonymous referees.

6 December 1991   James H. Fetzer

Science does not rest upon rock-bottom. The bold structure of its theories rises, as it were, above a swamp. It is like a building erected on piles. The piles are driven down from above into the swamp, but not down into any natural or "given" base; and when we cease our attempts to drive our piles into a deeper layer, it is not because we have reached firm ground. We simply stop when we are satisfied that they are firm enough to carry the structure, at least for the time being.

Karl R. Popper (1965).

CHAPTER ONE

WHAT IS SCIENCE?

This chapter provides a brief sketch of the history of science before turning to matters of methodology. The distinction between science as a descriptive inquiry and philosophy as a normative inquiry lays a foundation for considering the nature of explication in philosophy.

THE HISTORY AND PHILOSOPHY OF SCIENCE

This section sketches the history of physics and astronomy, while drawing a distinction between "cosmogonies," as stories that explain the unfamiliar by means of the familiar, and "cosmologies," as theories that explain the familiar by means of the unfamiliar.

Human beings have sought to understand the world around them from very early times. The records of ancient cultures are characterized by the myths that they embraced, including Babylonian, Egyptian, Hebrew, and Greek myths. Their study provides fascinating insights into early efforts to make the world a kinder and gentler, less threatening and more promising, place in which to live (Munitz 1957). The primary function of myth must have been to provide a framework relating human beings to a world that they found to be extremely difficult, if not impossible, to understand.

The earliest myths were anthropomorphic in their character in attributing human personalities and human characteristics to other-than-human things. Changes in the weather, lightning and thunder, seemed somehow less menacing when they could be understood as diverse manifestations of wars between gods. These gods themselves were modeled after humans, with similar traits of courage or cowardice, of knowledge or ignorance, of love and hate. They were persons with exaggerated powers and abilities.

The history of human efforts to secure an understanding of the world exhibits many twists and turns. Indeed, there appear to have been four main stages in the emergence of *cosmologies* as rational or scientific theories or accounts of the structure of the universe from *cosmogonies* as mythical accounts or stories of the nature of the world (Munitz 1957, pp. 1–2):

First, the transition from mythical cosmogonies (Babylonian, Egyptian, Hebrew, Greek) to rational speculations of the Ionian Nature Philosophers (Thales, Anaximander, Anaximines) and, especially, of the Pythagoreans.

Second, the emergence during the classical period in Greek philosophy of the geocentric and finite cosmologies of Plato and Aristotle and the astronomical tradition reflected by Ptolemy, where Earth plays a central role.

Third, the gradual transformation from the late middle ages to the early modern period, under the influence of the work of Copernicus, Kepler, and Galileo, to its synthesis by Newton, where the Sun plays a central role.

Fourth, the recent emergence of cosmological schemes incorporating the ideas of Einstein in support of the conception of a finite but unbounded and expanding universe, where neither the Earth nor the Sun play a central role.

The transition from the first to the second stage was primarily an *intellectual change* in the kinds of questions asked and in the kinds of answers given. When Thales of Miletus (?640–546 B.C.) suggested that everything is (made of) water, he initiated a nonmythical tradition searching for general answers about everything in terms of causal, physical, or structural properties. His was a plausible position to maintain, not least of all because water occurs as a solid, as a liquid, and as a gas, but because it is indispensable to life and there is a lot of it around. There was evidence for Thales' position. __

Thales was succeeded by Anaximander of Miletus (611–547 B.C.), who advanced the theory that water could not be the stuff of which all things are made (because it, too, must be explained), but rather the Boundless (or "Infinite"), conceived as an eternal, imperishable substance of which all things are made and back to which all things must return. Anaximander also proposed a cosmology according to which the Sun is like a chariot wheel with a hollow rim that is full of fire, suspended in space (Kuhn 1957, p. 26). And he believed that humans, like other animals, were originally a kind of fish.

Anaximines of Miletus (c 550 B.C.) thought that his teacher, Anaximander, was right in thinking there is a lot of this stuff around, but wrong in thinking it was the Boundless. In its place he proposed air, vapor, or mist, which animates and extends infinitely throughout space. Everything else arises from a process of rarefaction and condensation, where air, when rarefied, becomes fire, and, when condensed, it becomes in turn wind, cloud, water, earth, and stone. Taking air as the basic stuff was regressive, but a causal mechanism to explain observable differences was a great advance.

Pythagoras (c 530 B.C.) was enormously important for maintaining that everything is formed of numbers. Numbers are, for the Pythagoreans, the principles of things, not as being the stuff of which all things are made but rather as constituting their formal or their relational structure. While the Pythagoreans endowed certain numbers with almost mystical significance, the importance of their interest in numbers derives from their efforts to discover a numerical orderliness beneath the surface of phenomena, thus contributing to the idea of mathematical laws that govern every process.

The intellectual difference involved in the transition from the first to the second stage might therefore be said to represent the difference between "stories" and "theories." Cosmogonies as *stories* tend to assume the form of a narrative with an historical and a sequential character, where the subjects are particular things, including specific gods and people. Cosmologies as *theories*, by comparison, tend to assume the form of general propositions that are structural and relational and sometimes also causal. They appear to represent very different kinds of questions and answers.

The transition from the second to the third stage, by comparison, was strongly affected by a *technological innovation*, the telescope, especially in the hands of Galileo. This instrument enabled a student of nature to make empirical discoveries that were impossible in its absence. Indeed, the transition from the third to the fourth stage seems to be all the more striking as a consequence of *theoretical speculations* by Einstein that led to the conception of frames of reference and of the relativity of motion, which placed classical mechanics into new perspective as a special case.

One of the most fascinating differences between cosmogonies as stories and cosmologies as theories can be discerned from the perspective of what might be called their respective explanatory strategies. As Milton Munitz (Munitz 1957, p. 5) observes, mythical stories tend to exhibit the pattern of *explaining the unfamiliar by means of the familiar*. The world tends to be viewed as the art work or product of a creative artisan, as a biological organism on a par with a living human being, and as dutifully obeying or willfully disobeying the dictates of a supreme father-figure or law-giver.

But as Karl R. Popper (1968, p. 102) has emphasized, scientific theories tend to exhibit the pattern of *explaining the familiar by means of the unfamiliar*. The atomic theory of matter, which characterizes elements of different kinds by means of the properties of the atoms and molecules of which all things are made, would appear to be an appropriate illustration. Familiar substances, such as water, are understood as composed of atoms of hydrogen and oxygen, which are made up of protons, electrons, and neutrons, where the existence of these unfamiliar and nonobservable entities provides a possible explanation for their observable and familiar behavior.

What can be seen from even a sketch of the emergence of cosmology from cosmogony is the successive displacement of human beings as the center of a mythical universe inhabited by gods, of the Earth as the center of the planetary system and of the Sun as the center of the physical universe in favor of a conception of the world as finite, but boundless and expanding. The growth of science, it appears, may bring an increased understanding of the natural world, but it does not thereby enhance the place of human beings within the natural order. The opposite seems far closer to the mark.

THE AIM OF SCIENCE

This section considers differences between science and religion. It suggests that science aims at the discovery of laws of nature, which can provide a foundation for empirically testable explanations. And it hints that science is descriptive, while philosophy is prescriptive.

This may be thought to explain at least in part a persistent tendency toward religious belief. If science makes human beings less comfortable and more estranged from the world, perhaps religion can make us feel more comfortable and less estranged. There is no inherent tension, after all, between belief in an omnipotent, omniscient, divine creator and the study of laws of nature. If God knows everything and can do anything, then creating a world that operates by means of natural laws would be within its power. The study of science could be the study of God's will.

The potential for conflict between religious belief and scientific view arises when one is mistaken for the other. A feature that distinguishes between them is that religious beliefs are typically "matters of faith," in the sense that they do not require grounds, reasons, or evidence in their support. Scientific beliefs, by contrast, are typically "matters of reason," in the sense that they do require grounds, reasons, or evidence—often of very precise kinds—in their support. So long as matters of faith are not confounded with matters of reason, they might survive without conflict.

But while religious beliefs and scientific beliefs do not have to stand in opposition, the "history of warfare" between science and religion suggests that they sometimes do (White 1955). The Bishops of Padua, for example, refused to peer through Galileo's telescope, because they knew already—without the benefit of observations by means of instruments—how the Moon should look. What tends to separate science from religion in resolving disputes thus appears to be its reliance upon observation and experimentation for the empirical resolution of conflicting beliefs.

Thomas S. Kuhn, for example, whose views we are going to explore, has suggested that, while cosmogonies may be psychologically satisfying, cosmologies must be not only psychologically satisfying but also provide *empirically testable explanations* for observable phenomena, frequently in considerable detail (Kuhn 1957, pp. 6–7). Precisely what makes a position "empirically testable" might be difficult to say, since even thunder and lightning could be advanced as "evidence" that the gods are angry. But there is no reason to doubt that Kuhn's insight is on the right track.

The objectivity to which science aspires is defined by intersubjective standards of reasoning. In principle, different scientists confronted by the same alternative hypotheses and the same relevant evidence would tend to accept and reject all and only the same tentative conclusions by virtue of relying upon the same principles of reasoning. Whether or not this conception of scientific objectivity can be sustained is one that we shall consider in this book. But it should be obvious already that an attitude of this kind is unlikely to be displayed in cases of conflicting faiths.

Indeed, when we encounter the difficult problems that are posed by indeterministic processes within the quantum domain, the psychological function that Kuhn describes may be called into question as an essential feature of a scientific theory (or "conceptual scheme"), because specific theories that seem to be theoretically adequate and experimentally confirmed also appear to be psychologically unsatisfying for scientists who are used to dealing with deterministic processes in the classical domain. This is but one of many issues to which we shall have occasion to return.

Among the benefits of studying the history of science appears to be the support that it provides for the conception of empirical science as aimed at the discovery of *laws of nature*. From this point of view, one of the most striking figures in the history of thought turns out to have been Heraclitus of Ephesus (c 540–475 B.C.), who maintained that everything is in flux: "You can never step into the same river twice!"

What is most important about Heraclitus for us is his view that cosmic processes are not haphazard or arbitrary but governed by underlying *logos* or law.

Given the conception of science as aimed at the discovery of laws of nature, the history of science can be viewed as an effort to reconstruct the attempts of scientists in the past to discover those laws, and the philosophy of science can be viewed as an effort to reconstruct how science itself could possibly succeed. If science seeks to discover laws that are true of (or "model") the world and the history of science describes past attempts to discover those laws, then the philosophy of science attempts to discover a model by means of which science might best be understood.

There may be those who think that the very distinction between science and the philosophy of science is fundamentally misconceived. "Why not just let scientists speak for themselves?", you may ask. And, indeed, this is a very good question. Almost every living scientist has an opinion about the nature of his discipline. Accounts of science by scientists may be found in many books and are advanced in many lectures. Frequently they subscribe to what is often said to be the "inductivist" conception of science, but sometimes they endorse the "deductivist" conception instead.

The *inductivist conception* of science envisions science as a process of several successive steps, such as those of Observation, Classification, Generalization, and Prediction. A rule of reasoning commonly associated with this view is known as the *straight rule* of enumerative induction, namely:

(SR) If m/n observed As are Bs, infer (inductively) that m/n As are Bs,

provided, of course, that a suitable number of As have been observed under suitably varied conditions. A special case occurs if every observed A is a B (when $m = n$), where the inference to draw is that every A is a B.

The *deductivist conception* of science, by comparison, envisions science as a process of several different steps, such as Conjecture, Derivation, Experimentation, and Elimination. A rule of reasoning commonly associated with this view is the deductive rule of inference known as *modus tollens*:

(MT) Given 'if *p* then *q*' and 'not-*q*', infer (deductively) 'not-*p*',

where "*p*" stands for some specific theory and "*q*' " stands for the results of suitably conducted observations or experiments. When "*p*" is a statistical (or "probabilistic") theory, the inferential situation will be more complex.

The inductivist and the deductivist conceptions qualify as two models of science. Since they are intended to capture how science may properly be pursued and understood, it will be crucial for us to consider whether or not science could possibly succeed were its methods confined to those specified by each model. This is not a question of popularity. Even if one of these models were universally endorsed, that would not show that science thus conceived can succeed. And these are not the only alternatives.

It is fascinating to realize that a person's conception of the beginning of science presupposes a conception of the nature of science. Popper, for example, who is strongly identified with the deductivist conception, believes that Parmenides of Elea (c 515–? B.C.) formulated the first deductive theory (of the universe as one big block of unchanging matter), an hypothesis that Democritus (?470–?400 B.C.) subsequently rejected on the basis of the observed phenomenon of motion, which Parmenides' view implied was impossible (Popper 1968, p. 146). For Popper empirical science begins here.

An inductivist, however, might maintain that Popper is mistaken, because the crucial procedures of science are activities that depend not upon the deductive principle, *modus tollens*, but on the inductive principle, the straight rule. An approach that emphasizes the explanation of the familiar by means of the unfamiliar, of course, might view Anaximander as the first scientist, since he explained the visible by means of the invisible. Alternatively, the idea of unchanging laws that lie behind changing phenomena might function as a rationale for looking to Heraclitus instead.

THE NATURE OF EXPLICATIONS

Several different modes of definition are considered: ostensive definition, nominal definition, meaning analysis, empirical analysis, explication, and implicit definition. The conception of philosophy as an explicative activity provides a solution for "the paradox of analysis."

Different scientists say different things about the nature of their discipline, yet it would not settle the matter even if they all agreed. Indeed, since both approaches have convinced adherents within the scientific community, we are going to give them both a serious hearing as we proceed. Moreover, it should come as no surprise if the pursuit of science and the pursuit of philosophy of science require diverse backgrounds and abilities. There is no more reason to think those who excel at one of these activities must also excel at the other than there is in the case of actors and critics.

But if the nature of science is not a matter that can be decided within the scientific community by a majority vote, you might also wonder how, if at all, such questions could be settled. The answer turns out to be that theorizing about science shares certain properties in common with theorizing about nature, except that the difference between the descriptive and the normative makes a major difference. We are pursuing a rather special kind of definition. In order to understand what is involved, therefore, we must consider the nature of words and how they can obtain any meaning.

A definition is a linguistic entity that has two linguistic parts, namely: its *definiendum*, which consists of the word, phrase, or expression to be defined, and its *definiens*, which is some word, phrase, or expression by means of which it is defined. A standard symbol for displaying a definition is ". . . =df ____," which means ". . . means by definition ____". Thus,

(DF) bachelor =df unmarried, adult male.

This implies that the word, phrase, or expression that fills in the ". . ." slot has the same meaning as the word, phrase, or expression that fills in the "＿＿" slot. These terms thus become synonymous by definition.

There are at least two immediate problems with definitions. One is that the same words, phrases, or expressions might occur with different meanings in different languages. When we fail to appreciate the difference, linguistic confusions might result. The other is that the undefined (or "primitive") elements of a language cannot possess their meaning by means of definition, which generates the problem of primitives. Here I will follow the usual practice and let it go for now. This issue is investigated in Fetzer (1991a), however, and we shall return to it in Chapter Eight.

To provide one illustration of how it might be possible to acquire the use of words or learn their meaning without already knowing the meaning of other words, consider *ostensive definition*. Words are "defined" ostensively by displaying samples or examples of the kind of thing that is thereby being defined. The meaning of the word "pencil," for example, might be explained by exhibiting some pencils to someone. The risk involved here, of course, is that properties of those specific things (such as their color, size, or shape) may be mistaken for those of every such thing.

Carl G. Hempel has distinguished four species of definition (Hempel 1952, pp. 1–14), the first of which is *nominal definition*. A nominal definition occurs when some new word, phrase, or expression is introduced as having the same meaning as some old word, phrase, or expression. He introduces the word "tiglon" as meaning the offspring of a male tiger and a female lion, where the acceptability of this definition is only a matter of agreement between the members of a language-using community. The definiendum and the definiens thus have the same meaning simply as a result of stipulation.

The second species discussed by Hempel is *meaning analysis*. A meaning analysis provides a report upon the established usage of a word, phrase or expression within a language-using community. Since linguistic practices may differ from one community to another and from time to time, they are relative to those communities and times. The word "fuzz," for example, was slang for policemen or officers of the law to street gangs in New York during the 1960s.

Although Hempel suggests that these definitions can be validated by reflection upon their meaning, a sentence that formulates a meaning analysis will either be true or be false insofar as it provides an accurate or inaccurate reflection of the linguistic practices of the community and time.

The third species that Hempel discusses is *empirical analysis*. An empirical analysis may occur when some samples or examples of the kind of thing under consideration are available for examination, which can afford an enhanced understanding of things of that kind. Stuff of the kind *gold*, for example, was familiar to ancient peoples, who knew it was a yellowish, malleable metal. But they did not know that atoms of gold have the atomic number 79 as a function of the number of protons in the nucleus of atoms of that kind. This discovery, which did not occur until the nineteenth century, offered a foundation for redefining the meaning of "gold" by means of that property.

The fourth species that Hempel discusses is *explication*. The purpose of explication is to take a somewhat vague and ambiguous word, phrase or expression and subject it to critical scrutiny, where the result is a recommendation or proposal as to how it might best be understood in order to achieve certain theoretical or philosophical objectives. Words such as "science," "theory," and "law," for example, might be subject to explication in an attempt to develop a framework for better understanding the nature of science. Since explications have the character of suggestions, they can be qualified as more or less adequate, but they cannot be simply qualified as either true or false.

Hempel suggests three criteria that are relevant for evaluating the adequacy of definitions. The first is *syntactical determinacy*, in the sense that the grammatical character of the word, phrase, or expression under consideration must be rendered explicit. Surely we do not understand a term if we cannot identify its syntax. The second is *definitional relevance*, in the sense that some significant context of usage must be specifiable in which the defined term applies. There is no point in defining a term that has no use. The third is *theoretical significance*, in the sense that an adequate explication, in particular, ought to clarify and illuminate the meaning of the term within that context. An explication should advance our understanding.

Another mode of definition that deserves to be mentioned is that of *implicit definition*. An implicit definition occurs when a word, phrase, or expression is used within a specific theoretical context, where, even though no meaning is directly assigned to that word, phrase or expression, it assumes meaning indirectly through its inferential relations to other words, and so forth. Thus, although Newton declined to define the meaning of "gravity" ("I feign no hypotheses!"), that did not render the word meaningless, since it acquired indirect meaning through its linkage to Newton's various laws.

The modes of ostensive definition and of implicit definition indicate a point easily overlooked, namely: that some kinds of definition are modes of "definition" only in a very broad sense. Since definitions, strictly understood, relate one linguistic entity to another as "having the same meaning," neither ostensive definitions (which relate words and things) nor implicit definitions (which relate words and inferences) entirely qualify as *modes of definition*. Perhaps the most important among them all from the point of view of our investigation, however, is the mode known as "explication."

Among the virtues of Hempel's conception of explication is that it provides a resolution of the "paradox of analysis," according to which philosophy itself is misconceived as an attempt to match definienda with corresponding definiens. For if we know what we are talking about, we already know which definiens corresponds to the definiendum under consideration, in which case it is unnecessary. But if we don't know what we are talking about, then we are in no position to match definiendum with definiens, in which case it is impossible. What we have discovered is that we can partially or vaguely understand what we are talking about and proceed from there.

THE ANALYSIS OF LANGUAGE

Logical empiricism combined Humean empiricism with the logical analysis of language. It refined Hume's distinction of "relations between ideas" and "matters of fact" by employing an abstract model of a language (a "language framework") as a technique for analyzing language.

Without doubt, those who committed themselves most wholeheartedly to the methodology of explication in their effort to understanding empirical science were members of the twentieth century movement known as *logical empiricism*. This approach, which was developed especially in the work of Hans Reichenbach, Rudolf Carnap, and Carl G. Hempel, among others, agrees that empirical science has the objective of discovering natural laws that are suitable for the explanation and the prediction of the occurrence of particular events. But it goes further in adopting specific views about the nature of scientific knowledge and the conditions of adequacy for adequate philosophical explications.

The *empirical* element of logical empiricism was profoundly affected by the philosophical views of David Hume (1711–1776). Hume drew a distinction between knowledge of "matters of fact," on the one hand, and knowledge of "relations between ideas," on the other. Hume's view was that all knowledge of *matters of fact* had to be traceable to "impressions" derived from experience. Ideas that could be traced back to impressions in experience that gave rise to them were permissible, legitimate, or acceptable (from the point of view of the theory of knowledge), but those that could not be so traced back were impermissible, illegitimate, and unacceptable.

Knowledge of *relations between ideas*, however, was a somewhat different story. Suppose you had acquired the idea of a chair ostensively through exposure to various examples of things called "chairs." Perhaps you thereby formed the idea that chairs are sometimes, but not always, made of wood. In this case, the idea that every chair is either made of wood or not would turn out to be something that could be known apart from experience. Such relations between ideas could be known without experience once those ideas themselves had been acquired by experience.

Perhaps the most important element of Hume's theory of knowledge is the contention that knowledge about the world can only be acquired on the basis of experience. No knowledge about the world, he maintained, can be obtained independently of experience. Knowledge obtained independently of experience, therefore, cannot be knowledge about the world. There may be knowledge that is independent of experience, including knowledge of relations between (combinations of various) ideas, but it cannot be informative about the world. This thesis would be essential to logical empiricism.

The *logical* element of logical empiricism derived from a methodological commitment to what is known as formal logic. An explication would not be accepted as "adequate" unless it could be fully formalized using what is called extensional logic (see below), especially the resources of predicate calculus. This condition of adequacy went beyond Hempel's syntactical determinacy requirement by restricting the syntax of acceptable explications to specific forms. Thus, in place of Hume's emphasis upon ideas in the mind, they placed emphasis upon words in a language, using modern logic as a framework for attacking philosophical problems.

Recasting Humean empiricism in a more sophisticated form, the logical empiricists thus refined Hume's notions of "relations between ideas" and "matters of fact" in relation to a language L, where sentences in lieu of ideas became the focus of attention. A sentence would now be said to be *analytic* when its truth follows from the definitions and grammar of that language alone, and *synthetic* when its truth does not follow from L alone. In relation to a language L, the truth of an analytic sentence can be known *a priori* (independent of experience), while the truth of a synthetic sentence could only be discovered *a posteriori* (on the basis of experience).

The result of their efforts was an imposing intellectual edifice founded on three crucial elements: the analytic/synthetic distinction, an observational/theoretical distinction, and a methodological commitment to extensional logic as the appropriate framework for philosophical investigations. The elaboration of this position required a defense of its basic ingredients, including the problem of accounting for how analytic knowledge could be justified. This prospect, after all, hinges upon the possibility of acquiring knowledge of the grammar and the vocabulary of a specific language L.

Carnap was especially resourceful in pursuing formal methods for understanding language (Carnap 1939, pp. 3–16). The distinction between syntax, semantics, and pragmatics was enormously important, because it supplied the foundation for understanding the construction of a *language framework* (or of an artificial language) that corresponds to but does not duplicate a specific language. Thus, the construction of a model **M** of language **L** is a process that begins with pragmatic observations of linguistic usage within a specific community as its raw data and proceeds to reconstruct its semantical and its syntactical rules by a process of abstraction.

The notion of abstraction was important here, because it meant that a model **M** of language **L** would provide a simplified construction, which might clarify and illuminate some features of that language while obscuring and distorting others. Certain decisions, such as whether or not specific ambiguities, slang expressions, informal conventions, and such, which obtain in **L,** would be preserved must be made in constructing the model **M.** The features that were retained would be illuminated by having their relations to other features emphasized by the process of abstraction, but the absence of other features from the model would thereby distort them.

Carnap advanced a lucid conception of a model of kind **M** as consisting of a grammar **G** and a vocabulary **V,** where **M** $=<$**G, V**$>$. The vocabulary **V** consists of the logical signs **LS** and the nonlogical signs **NLS,** including the names and predicates of the language, while the grammar **G** consists of formation rules **FR** and transformation rules **TR.** The function of the transformation rules is to govern what follows from what (as deductive rules of inference), while the function of the formation rules is to provide recursive methods to determine which strings of signs of the vocabulary qualify as the well-formed formulae (or the "sentences") of the language.

The formation and transformation rules that Carnap employed were completely *extensional* (or "truth-functional") in character. This means that the truth-values of any sentences that are constructed out of other sentences are completely determined by the truth-values of their component sentences. Sentences are divided into "molecular" and "atomic," where molecular sentences have other sentences as parts, while atomic sentences do not. What makes sentences "truth-functional" is that the logical form of molecular sentences guarantees their truth-values are completely determined by those of their atomic sentence components.

Atomic sentences of the logical form, '. . . *n* is ＿＿*p*', where '. . . *n*' is replaced by a name and '＿＿ *p*' by a predicate, will be *true* if the thing named by the name has the property designated by the predicate, but otherwise are false. Molecular sentences of the form 'not-＿＿*s*' are true if sentence '＿＿*s*' is not true but otherwise are false; of the form '*s*1 or *s*2' are true when either '*s*1' is true or '*s*2' is true or both but otherwise are not; of the form '*s*1 and *s*2' when both '*s*1' is true and '*s*2' is true but otherwise not; and so forth, for all possible combinations of truth values.

Consider, for example, the sentence, "John is tall." This sentence will turn out to be true if the thing named by the name "John" has the property designated by the predicate "is tall," but otherwise is false. Since "John is tall" is an atomic sentence, a molecular sentence built out of it, such as "It is not the case that John is tall" (or "John is not tall") will be true just in case its atomic component, "John is tall," is false but otherwise will be false. Sentences of other molecular forms, of course, could be built out of various combinations of atomic or molecular sentences.

THE ANALYTIC AND THE SYNTHETIC

Having recast Hume's distinction of "relations between ideas" and "matters of fact" into one between analytic and synthetic sentences, logical empiricism was threatened by Quine's denial that such a distinction could be justified, which appeared to undermine its position.

Within this formal framework, a narrow distinction between analytic and synthetic sentences could easily be drawn by maintaining that sentences whose truth follows from their logical form alone are *analytic* in relation to **M** (or "analytic-in-**M**"), while sentences whose truth does not follow from their logical form alone are *synthetic* in relation to **M** ("synthetic-in-**M**"). Since these distinctions apply exclusively to "sentences" as sequences of signs that are either true or false (a requirement called the law of excluded middle) and not both true and false (called the law of non-contradiction), this approach appears to have its intended effect.

The difference between analytic and synthetic sentences could now be formally displayed. Sentences of the form, 's or not-s', will turn out to be always true, while those of the form, 's and not-s', will turn out to be always false. This was not hard to demonstrate using "truth-tables":

(TT)	(A)	s	(B) not-s	(C) s or not-s	(D) s and not-s
	(1)	T	F	T	F
	(2)	F	T	T	F

Thus, any sentence of form (C) must always be true, because if 's' is true, then 'not-s' must be false, but if 's' is false, then 'not-s' must be true. Since any sentence of the form, 's or not-s', is true if one or the other is true, when understood truth-functionally, it must be true.

Similarly, any sentence of form (D) must always be false, because if 's' is true, then 'not-s' must be false, but if 's' is false, then 'not-s' must be true. Since any sentence of the form, 's and not-s', is true if and only if both its component sentences are true, when understood truth-functionally, it must be false. These are very simple examples, of course, where sentences whose logical form guarantees their truth ("John is a bachelor or John is not a bachelor") are called "tautologies," and sentences whose logical form guarantees their falsity ("John is a bachelor and John is not a bachelor") are labelled as "contradictions."

The truth-functional interpretation of ". . . or ____," ". . . and ____," and so forth thus supported the finding that some sentences are true and others are false on logical grounds alone (or "L-true" and "L-false", respectively). If definitions such as (DF) are features of a language **L,**

(DF) bachelor = df unmarried, adult male,

however, then the conception of analytic sentences as those that are L-true could be broadened to include those that turn out to be L-true when definiens are substituted for definiendum. A sentence such as,

(S1) A bachelor is unmarried,

for example, could be shown to be analytic by such a substitution, since,

(S2) An unmarried adult male is unmarried,

follows from (S1) by substitution and can readily be shown to be L-true.

Let us assume that 'Bx' stands for 'x is a bachelor' while 'Ux', 'Ax', and 'Mx' stand for 'x is unmarried', 'x is an adult', and 'x is male', respectively. Let us also assume that a sentence of the form, 'if ____$s1$ then ____$s2$', interpreted truth-functionally, has the same meaning as a sentence of the form, 'either not-____$s1$ or $s2$', where 'if . . . then ____' sentences of this kind are known as "material conditionals." This interpretation supports the rule,

(MP) Given 'if p then q' and 'p', infer (deductively) 'q',

which is known as *modus ponens*, in addition to the rule *modus tollens*.

We know by (DF) that 'Bx' may be replaced by 'Ux and Ax and Mx'. This means 'Bx if and only if Ux and Ax and Mx' is true, where '. . . if and only if ____' implies that both sentences have the same truth value and can replace each other in any extensional (truth-functional) context. To show that (S1) "A bachelor is unmarried" (that is, 'if Bx then Ux') cannot be false and is therefore analytic in the broad sense, assume 'Bx' and derive 'Ux'. But 'Ux and Ax and Mx' follows immediately from (DF) and 'Bx' by substitution. And 'Ux' follows from 'Ux and Ax and Mx' by the truth-functional definition of '. . . and ____'. Hence, given (DF), (S1) has the same meaning as (S2) "An unmarried adult male is unmarried" and cannot possibly be false. Therefore, (S1) is analytic in the broad sense.

This approach thus appeared to vindicate the logical empiricist conception that some kinds of knowledge can be established *a priori*, since some sentences are analytic. Some are logical truths that are true on the basis of their logical form alone and are known as tautologies. They are "analytic" in the narrow sense. Others are true by definition and are not logical truths but are reducible to logical truths by substitution of definiens for definiendum. These are "analytic" in the broad sense. Thus, any sentence could be said to be "analytic" (or "analytic-in-**L**") when its truth follows from the grammar and the vocabulary of the language **L** alone as long as the vocabulary is viewed as including definitions of form (DF).

It therefore came as quite a shock when the well-known logician, W. V. O. Quine, published "Two Dogmas of Empiricism," which is one of the most influential papers by any contemporary philosopher (Quine 1953). Quine challenges the analytic/synthetic distinction as "a metaphysical article of faith" on the ground that the alleged distinction has never been completely justified. He cites four notions that have been employed in its defense—those of definition, analyticity, interchangeability, and semantic rule—contending that none of them can do without appeal to prior notions of analyticity and synonymy. His critique of a second "dogma" (of reductionism) is a matter to which I shall return in Chapter Three. For the present, I want to explore some questions concerning Quine's attack on the first dogma.

We know that definitions relate one linguistic entity to another linguistic entity. The notion of analyticity, as we have already discovered, is indeed intimately connected to the notions of definition and interchangeability. Sentences that are analytic in the broad sense, after all, are those that are reducible to logical truths by the interchange of a definiens for its definiendum. Semantic rules are exemplified by lists of pairs of words as having the same meaning or as sharing parts of their meaning and can be formalized by means of their logical relations. However, in Quine's view, all these approaches depend upon and presuppose prior relations of synonymy, the existence of which no philosopher ought to take for granted.

Yet Quine concedes a great deal along the way. He admits that there are some sentences whose truth or falsity is a function of their grammatical form alone, the logical truths. He acknowledges that there are some forms of definition, such as nominal definition, that are unobjectionable for the purpose of abbreviation. Relative to Hempel's framework, therefore, Quine's attack appears directed against meaning analyses, empirical analyses, and explications. But explications are not suitable objects of his criticism, since, as recommendations, they do not pretend to reflect previously existing relations of synonymy between definiens and definiendum. Indeed, even empirical analyses appear to be immune from his criticism.

Since Quine concedes analyticity for logical truths and for nominal definitions, he endorses the distinction for syntactical truths and for at least one kind of semantical truths. If he is contending that meaning analyses and empirical analyses are results of empirical inquiry and can never be known with certainty, his position is right but is hardly surprising. Since Carnap has elaborated how to construct a model M for a language L, the analytic/synthetic distinction can still be drawn in relation to M if not in relation to L, where M is understood as an explication of L. But if this is the case, then what Quine is really rejecting is the method of explication.

Quine discusses explication, but he imposes the condition that an explication qualifies as adequate when the explicated word, phrase, or expression has the same meaning "taken as a whole" within the context of its antecedent usage (Quine 1953, p. 25). Such a condition, however, appears to be reasonable only provided ordinary and scientific discourse is never vague or ambiguous when "taken as a whole." Surely that is asking for more than might rationally be required. (Indeed, it is even incompatible with Quine's thesis of the indeterminacy of translation, a matter to which we shall return in Chapter Eight.) In spite of its enormous influence, Quine's critique of analyticity seems to be difficult to sustain.

Quine closes his essay with a famous passage in which he describes the physical objects that are posited by the conceptual schemes of scientific theories "as irreducible posits comparable, epistemologically, to the gods of Homer" (Quine 1953, p. 44). He concedes that he believes in physical objects and not in Homer's gods, but maintains that their difference is only a matter of degree, where the myth of physical objects has proven to be "more efficacious" in supporting successful systems for coping with experience. The differences between myths and theories, however, may actually run much deeper than Quine appears willing to admit.

In spite of its plausibility, Quine's attack upon the analytic/synthetic distinction is only forceful when definitions are supposed to reflect previously existing relations of synonymy, a condition that explications, especially, do not satisfy. As a result, it cannot be sustained.

CHAPTER TWO

LAWS AND LAWLIKENESS

*E*mpirical science attempts to discover a synthetic model (theory) of the world, but philosophy of science tries to discover an analytic (explicative) model of science. The most important task connecting them is to arrive at a suitable view of the nature of laws of nature.

LAWLIKE VS. ACCIDENTAL GENERALIZATIONS

Myths and theories both assume a conditional relationship between certain conditions and specific events, but mythical "explanations," unlike scientific explanations, appear to have a low degree of empirical testability. The concept of a "theory square" clarifies this issue.

The most important difference between myths and theories emerges from the perspective of the kinds of explanations that they provide. The behavior of the world at the hands of the gods, including their use of lightning and thunder as weapons in their battles, for example, would enable us to anticipate the occurrence of lightning and thunder *if we could predict the behavior of the gods themselves*, but otherwise does not. What it would take to convert myths about gods into scientific theories would be the availability of evidence indicating when the gods are going to behave one way (lightning and thunder) rather than another (clear and sunny).

Myth and theories may both assume the existence of conditional relationships between different occurrences. Myths maintaining that lightning and thunder are indications that the gods are angry can be translated as conditional hypotheses asserting, *if* the gods are angry, *then* thunder and lightning will occur. Theories maintaining that lightning and thunder are indications of low pressure and static electricity can be translated as conditional hypotheses asserting that, *if* low pressure and static electricity are present, *then* thunder and lightning will occur. The difference is that we have methods for measuring the presence or the absence of low pressure and static electricity but not of whether the gods are angry or not.

Quine could adhere to the position that the differences at stake here are matters of degree rather than of kind. In relation to Kuhn's emphasis upon empirically testable explanations, Quine could maintain that myths appealing to gods are "explanations" that simply have a low degree of testability. Some *differences of degree*, however, are sufficiently important as to qualify properly as *differences in kind*. What Quine appears to be missing here is the ingredient of lawfulness that appears to be indispensable to scientific theories. The conception of occurrences as manifestations of laws of nature that might be both testable and explanatory seems to be absent from view.

We have already adopted the position that empirical science aims at the discovery of natural laws, which receives ample support from histories of science, such as Kuhn (1957) and Cohen (1960). What we do not yet know, however, is what it takes for something to be a law of nature. Moreover, there appear to be at least two aspects to this problem. On the one hand, we want to know the kind of thing that laws of nature are supposed to be, which is a question of *ontology*. On the other hand, we want to know how knowledge of laws of nature might be acquired if laws of nature are things of that kind, which is a question of *epistemology*. Both are crucial matters, but epistemic problems appear to presuppose solutions to ontic problems.

The differences involved here may be displayed by appealing to what may be referred to as a "theory square." Speaking generally, natural laws relate properties to properties and events to events, where every instance of the reference property R (angry gods, gold thing, and so forth) is lawfully related to an attribute A (stormy weather, malleability, and so on). The ontic problem is to understand the nature of these properties and the character of the relation between them. In order to discover which hypotheses are true, however, there must also be some suitable conditions under which it would be possible, in principle, to tell whether these properties and relations are present or absent. The epistemic problem, therefore, is to understand how lawful hypotheses can be subjected to relevant empirical tests.

If we assume that the presence or absence of the reference property R under specific test conditions and presence or absence of attribute A can be similarly ascertained under other specific test conditions, then the following diagram (or "theory square") reflects the range of issues involved here:

Property [R] is related by law to attribute [A]

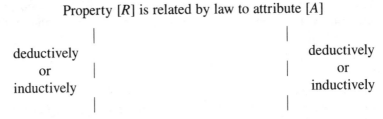

<table>
<tr><td>deductively
or
inductively</td><td></td><td>deductively
or
inductively</td></tr>
</table>

Empirical test for [R] is correlated with empirical test for [A]

Figure 1. A Theory Square

Thus, in relation to Figure 1, a complete theory of the character of lawful hypotheses would have to provide adequate answers to ontic questions about the nature of properties R and A and of the relations between them, on the one hand, and adequate answers to epistemic questions about correlations between empirical tests of those properties and their results, on the other.

As simple illustrations of the principal problems that are involved here, consider hypothesis $h1$: *everything gold is malleable*. If the attribute (being) *malleable* is related by law to the reference property (being) *gold*, then presumably $h1$ is a natural law. Or hypothesis $h2$: *all my friends are rich*. If the attribute (being) *rich* is related by law to the reference property (being) *my friend*, then presumably *h2* is a natural law. And so forth. Such an account would be complete only if it explained how the presence or absence of (being) *gold*/(being) *my friend/* . . . and the presence or absence of (being) *malleable*/(being) *rich/* . . . were related to suitable tests and outcomes, etc.

A difficulty emerges at this juncture, however, since some correlations between properties seem to be lawful but others do not. There might be a lawful correlation between things that are gold and things that are malleable, for example, but it is difficult to imagine that there could be a lawful relation between being my friend and being rich—even if all of my friends happened to be rich! In the remainder of this chapter, therefore, we shall focus upon the ontic problem of discovering what kind of relationship between properties makes relations lawful. And in the chapters that follow, we shall focus upon the epistemic problem of relating laws to experience.

According to a tradition with roots in ancient history, there are basic differences between laws of nature and laws of society, on the one hand, and between laws of nature and accidental generalizations, on the other. Laws of society can be violated and can be changed, while laws of nature can neither be violated nor be changed. Laws of nature are supposed to reflect *necessary connections* between properties or between events (where one event might be the cause of another as its effect), which are absent in the case of merely accidental generalizations. As a consequence, while all laws are true generalizations, not all true generalizations are laws.

Among Hume's contributions, however, was a critique of this conception on the basis of the epistemic principle that it is rational to accept the existence of properties and relations only when they are accessible to experience. According to Hume, necessary connections are nonobservable relations between various properties and events that are inaccessible to experience and cannot qualify as features of an acceptable conception of lawful relations, which should instead be restricted to constant conjunctions or relative frequencies between observable properties and events. Yet there are no differences between mere generalizations and genuine laws only if there are no differences between correlations and causation.

SUPPORT FOR COUNTERFACTUALS

Aristotle drew a distinction between lawful and accidental generalizations that appears to be excessively metaphysical. Hume allowed a distinction to be drawn, but it was unacceptably subjective. A partial solution can be found by appealing to subjunctive conditionality.

Aristotle (384–322 B.C.) appreciated this problem and distinguished between the "universal" properties and the "commensurately universal" properties of things (*Posterior Analytics*, I, 73a–74a). (Merely) universal properties are properties that everything of a certain kind happens to have but could continue to exist without. Commensurately universal properties, by comparison, are properties that everything of a certain kind have which they could not continue to exist without. For Aristotle, commensurately universal properties were essential properties, which occur in a proper definition of a thing of that kind. (Merely) universal properties, on his approach, are only accidental and are not definitional.

While Hume denied the existence of necessary connections in nature that relate properties to properties or causes to effects, he admitted the existence of habitual connections in the mind relating words to words or concepts to concepts. A consequence of his account was that natural laws, objectively considered, could consist of no more than constant conjunctions or relative frequencies, where our inevitable tendency to expect the occurrence of one event to attend the occurrence of another is nothing more than a habit of the mind, irresistible perhaps, but lacking in objective foundation.

Neither of these alternatives for understanding the nature of laws could have been very appealing to logical empiricists. Aristotle's conception was perceived as *excessively metaphysical* because it appeared to be very difficult to support the conception of essential properties. Moreover, these properties are related to reference properties by definition, which would make laws analytic rather than synthetic. Hume's account, however, made any differences between laws and non-laws depend upon the existence of a certain attitude, which made the distinction between them *unacceptably subjective*. Aristotle's theory was too strong, while Hume's was too weak.

The logical empiricists, who wanted a completely objective conception of natural laws, attempted to cast the problem as a matter of language. Using the resources of (first order) predicate calculus, they approached the issue as a question of logical form. A sentence S in a language L thus qualifies as a law in L if and only if S is lawlike and S is true, where the problem is reduced to the conditions required for a sentence to be lawlike in L. For S to be lawlike in L it must be unrestrictedly general in scope and have the capacity to support subjunctive conditionals in L, even though S is not true on syntactical or semantical grounds alone. (Thus, Hempel would propose that such sentences were expressed by means of purely qualitative predicates.)

An unrestricted generalization of the relevant kind assumes the form, 'For all x and all t, if x has property R at time t, then x has property A at t'. If the single arrow ". . . $\rightarrow$ _____" is used for the material conditional sign, then the logical form of a sentence of this kind can be specified as follows:

(UG-1) $(x)(t)(Rxt \rightarrow Axt)$.

Since the material conditional ". . . $\rightarrow$ _____" means the same thing as "either not- . . . or _____," by stipulation, a generalization of this kind will be true if everything in the world either does not have property R or has attribute A. If everything had a name, such as a, b, c, . . . , (UG-1) would be true in case either a does not have R or a has A and either b does not have R or b has A and . . . for as many things as there might happen to be in the world itself.

As it happens, however, this condition may be necessary for a generalization to be a law but it is not sufficient, because accidental generalizations can also satisfy this form. Suppose, for example, that every Corvette C (past, present, future) is painted red R. Then if everything were given a name as before, a, b, c, . . . , it would be true in each case that either a is not-C or a is R, either b is not-C or b is R, and so on. But that means the same thing as:

(UG-2) $(x)(t)(Cxt \rightarrow Rxt)$,

where (UG-2) has the same logical form as (UG-1). Yet even if this generalization were true, it would seem very odd to think that it should be a law.

Nelson Goodman pursued the objectives of this program with a serious study that had the unwanted effect of exposing the limits of extensional language for capturing the difference that is at stake here (Goodman 1947). A linguistic symptom of the difference between laws and non-laws seems to be that laws support subjunctive and counterfactual conditionals, while accidental generalizations do not. A *subjunctive* is an "if . . . then _____" in the subjunctive mood, which concerns what would happen if something were the case, by contrast with a material conditional, which concerns what is the case. Unlike material conditionals, subjunctives concern the way that things would be on the hypothetical assumption their antecedents are true. Subjunctive conditionals with false antecedents are called *counterfactuals*.

Goodman maintains that there is a strong connection between various recalcitrant problems concerning counterfactuals, dispositions, and laws of nature. Suppose, for example, that the generalization that (pure) gold is malleable *is* a law of nature. It then seems reasonable to make the subjunctive assertion of something *a* that, if it *were* gold, then it *would be* malleable, even when that something is a piece of chalk. Malleability itself, moreover, appears to be a dispositional property of things that are gold, since it characterizes certain ways that things would behave under certain specific conditions. These appear to be closely related problems.

Perhaps lawlike sentences might be limited to unrestrictedly general material conditionals that "support" corresponding subjunctives. Employing the double arrow ". . . $\Rightarrow$ _____" as the subjunctive condition sign, then a lawlike sentence could be (incompletely) described in the following way:

(UG-3) If '$(x)(t)(Rxt \rightarrow Axt)$' is a law, then '$(x)(t)(Rxt \Rightarrow Axt)$'.

Thus, if an unrestricted generalization, such as all Corvettes are red, did not support a corresponding subjunctive, such as (UG-4), it could not be a law:

(UG-4) $(x)(t)(Cxt \gg Rxt)$.

One difference between laws and accidental generalizations might be that, while both can satisfy (UG-1), only genuine laws can satisfy (UG-3) as well. But the problem still remains of explaining why those sentences are laws.

Goodman discusses attempts to resolve the problem by techniques that remain within the scope of extensional logic. Ultimately, however, he advocates a theory about the nature of laws that includes these two theses:

(T1) *lawlike generalizations are those on the basis of which we find ourselves willing to assert subjunctive and counterfactual conditionals*; and,

(T2) *lawlike generalizations are those we are willing to accept as true and project for unknown cases without having exhausted their instances.*

Indeed, the position that Goodman defends has been so influential that it has virtually defined the nature of the problem of law for other thinkers.

Contrary to (T1), however, logical truths and truths by definition both appear to be capable of sustaining subjunctive and counterfactual conditionals. Indeed, if "bachelor" equals by definition *unmarried adult male*, then surely for all x and all t, if x *were* a bachelor, then x *would be* male (adult, unmarried). Thus, if analytic sentences are represented as material conditionals preceded by the "□" as a sign of logical (or definitional) necessity, then any analytic sentence implies a corresponding subjunctive:

(GP-1) If '□(. . . → ____)', then '. . . $\gg$ ____'.

But this means that (T1) does not capture a property that is distinctive of lawlike sentences, which are meant to be both synthetic and *a posteriori*. (Yet even Hempel 1965, p. 272, envisions analytic sentences as lawlike!)

THE NEW RIDDLE OF INDUCTION

Goodman has suggested that there is a problem involving our choice of language in formulating predictions about the future, which has come to be known as "the problem of projectibility." There are reasons for thinking that it is not so serious as it is commonly supposed.

The problem with (T1) does not appear to be difficult to repair, since the requirement can be imposed that lawlike sentences are nonanalytic sentences that are capable of sustaining counterfactuals and subjunctives. Thus, a revised version of (UG-3) could be formulated that takes this problem into account by denying that analytic sentences could be laws:

(UG-5) If '$(x)(t)(Rxt \rightarrow Axt)$' is a law, then '$(x)(t)(Rxt \gg Axt)$' and it is not the case that '$\Box(x)(t)(Rxt \rightarrow Axt)$';

which makes nonanalyticity and support for subjunctives and counterfactuals necessary but not sufficient conditions for a sentence to be a law. (UG-5), like (UG-3), is still only a partial account, but it is less incomplete.

The problem with (T2) is more subtle but should not be assumed to be any less threatening. For Goodman's appeal to projectibility and confirmation by instances strongly suggests that he is proposing a pragmatic and epistemic solution for an ontic and semantic problem. Since laws are intended to describe properties and relations of the world, an adequate explication should make *what makes a law a law* properties and relations of the world. Hume's position does not satisfy this condition except by excluding our subjective expectations (or "habits of mind") from what it takes for something to be a law. If

Goodman is violating this condition, then his approach may provide the wrong kind of answer to the question.

The issues that we have considered to this point concern the nature of the relationship between the reference property R and the attribute A if that relationship is a lawful or a lawlike one. In other studies, however, Goodman contributes to the problem of understanding what kind of predicates or properties might function as reference properties or attributes (Goodman 1955). A complete analysis of lawlike sentences could satisfy the requirement of syntactical determinacy, after all, only by explaining the kinds of predicates that can occur within them as well as the kind of connection that must hold between them or else would be inadequate.

Goodman thereby introduced what is known as *the new riddle of induction* (or the "Goodman Paradox"), which is not the problem of counterfactual conditionals as such but rather the problem of projectible predicates (cf. Skyrms 1975). This difficulty arises from the notion that some predicates are suitable for making predictions about future cases, while others are not. "Blue" and "green" appear to be projectible, for example, but Goodman introduced a new family of predicates, such as "grue" and "bleen," which are definable by means of projectible predicates but do not appear to be projectible. The new riddle thus seems to be Hume's old problem of induction but appearing now in a new (linguistic) guise.

The old problem of induction concerns the rational justification of inferences about the future on the basis of regularities that have obtained in the past, when belief in necessary connections is no longer warranted. Thus, in order to appreciate their connection, we must consider the kind of predicates that Goodman introduces. A simple example of the problem might consist in reports about the color of emeralds, which have all been made prior to some time t, which, let us assume, might be midnight tonight. Even if all of the emeralds we have observed have been green, Goodman suggests, that affords no guarantee that they must remain that color in the future. Our evidence, for example, is consistent with the hypothesis that they might turn blue (or yellow, . . .) at midnight tonight.

Indeed, according to the straight rule, if m/n observed emeralds have been green, we should infer (inductively) that m/n emeralds are green, provided a suitable number have been observed under a wide variety of conditions (Salmon 1965). When every emerald that has been observed in the past is green, that principle supports the (inductive) inference that every emerald (past, present, future) is green and, therefore, that every emerald that will be observed in the future will be green. But Goodman has discovered that we may have been ignoring alternative hypotheses, such as that every emerald is grue, where something is *grue* just in case it is observed before time t and green or not observed before t and blue.

"Grue" itself, of course, is only an example of one member of a family of puzzling predicates. "Bleen" is another, where something is *bleen* just in case it is observed before t and blue or not observed before t and green. Indeed, the situation is compounded because ordinary predicates such as "green" and "blue" can be defined by means of the puzzling ones, where something is *blue* just in case it is observed before t and bleen but grue thereafter or something is *green* just in case it is observed before t and grue but bleen thereafter. From this viewpoint, Goodman's predicates appear to be on a par with the ordinary ones, which is difficult to explain.

Some thinkers have been led to draw the inference that "regularities" are subject to creation as well as to discovery, provided we are ingenious enough in constructing ways to describe the evidence, where "Whatever prediction you wish to make, a regularity can be found whose projection will license that prediction" (Skyrms 1975, p. 66–67). As a consequence, the prospects for an objective system of scientific reasoning of the kind described above—where different scientists confronted by the same alternative hypotheses and the same relevant evidence would tend to accept and reject all and only the same tentative conclusions by relying on the same principles of reasoning—may appear dim if not impossible.

The alternative remains, however, that the significance of Goodman's Paradox has been misunderstood. Consider, for example, that the time t that must be specified in the definition of a puzzling predicate is subject to variation. It could be midnight tonight, but it could also be midnight tomorrow night, or midnight last night. Or it might be 1 A.M. or 2 A.M. or 3 A.M. tonight or tomorrow or yesterday. Merely by setting a different time, each puzzling predicate can be converted into infinitely many. There is no single predicate that is "grue" but rather an infinite number of them, where each specifies a different time for such a change in color.

Consider further that the specific properties used to define these puzzling predicates might be arbitrarily associated with one another. Something could be defined as an *autow*, for example, just in case it is observed before time *t* and is an automobile but a cow thereafter, or is a *foxmallow* just in case it is observed before time *t* and a fox but a marshmallow thereafter. Surely the possibility of defining predicates in odd ways by incorporating a temporal ingredient and a change in state that occurs at that time does not mean that the world exhibits any such properties. There is no reason to think that there are any things of these odd kinds.

Indeed, the problem can be viewed as one of drawing an inference about a population based upon a sample. Every member of the population that belongs to the sample, let us assume, has been observed prior to some fixed time *t*. Members of the population that fall outside of the sample will be observed after that time or will remain unobserved forever. But surely we have no reason to think that things that have been green before *t* should be expected to change their color to blue (or else remain grue), since we have no reason to think time makes a difference.

Goodman thus appears to have introduced whole families of logically possible kinds of things that appear to have no instances. While the existence of things of odd kinds is clearly possible, there is no more reason to believe that anything is grue or bleen than there is to believe that anything is an autow or a foxmallow. Scientists, after all, are surely entitled to investigate hypotheses of various kinds—including those expressed in puzzling predicates—to ascertain whether or not the world is described thereby. If there are no things of the kinds described by these puzzling predicates, however, then any hypotheses expressed by means of them will remain as unsupported in the future as they have been in the past.

UNIVERSALS AND DISPOSITIONS

Even though Goodman's solution to the new riddle does not appear to hold the key to understanding the nature of laws of nature, it does invite attention to the kind of connection that obtains between properties when they are related by law and to their character as universals.

General principles of inductive inference likewise support the possibility that Goodman's Paradox has been widely misappraised. Carnap, for example, advanced the *requirement of total evidence* as a condition that must be satisfied by proper inductive reasoning (Carnap 1950, p. 211). According to Carnap's condition, inductive arguments have to be based on all of the available relevant evidence, where sentence *e* is relevant to hypothesis *h* just in case the truth or falsity of that sentence makes a difference to the truth or the falsity of that hypothesis. A sentence *e* whose truth or falsity makes no difference is not relevant to *h*.

In his most recent discussions of the problem of projectibility, Goodman maintains that a hypothesis is *projectible* only when it is supported, unviolated, and unexhausted by the available relevant evidence (Goodman 1985, p. 108). But this means that Goodman has not actually been solving the problem, *"What does it mean for a sentence to be lawlike?"*, but rather the different question, *"When are we entitled to regard a sentence as lawlike?"* And the answer that he offers is that we are entitled to regard a sentence as lawlike only when it satisfies certain conditions in relation to the available relevant evidence. Those are the hypotheses that are "projectible" and that support subjunctives and counterfactuals.

Indeed, Goodman's analysis of the fashion in which projectible hypotheses "support" subjunctive and counterfactual conditionals lends further credibility to the inference that he has not actually explained what it means for a sentence to be lawlike. The kind of "support" that Goodman has had in mind all along is that the projectible hypotheses are those on the basis of which *we find ourselves willing to assert* subjunctives and counterfactuals, which are those *we are willing to accept as true* and project for unknown cases without having exhausted their instances. If this is the case, however, then Goodman is apparently proposing an epistemic answer to an ontic question, which thereby commits a category mistake.

An historical and pragmatic solution of the kind that Goodman offers, of course, might be the best we can do, if the problem is so difficult that it cannot otherwise be resolved. Popper also views the problems of subjunctive conditionals, of dispositions, and of natural law as intimately interrelated, but he rejects an historical and pragmatic approach in favor of an ontological and semantical solution. For Popper, lawlike sentences describe *natural (or "physical") necessities*, which concern relations between universals. Universals, in turn, are understood as dispositions. Thus, on Popper's approach, subjunctives and counterfactuals can be explained as manifestations of natural necessities and of dispositions.

According to Popper's explication, natural or physical necessities are described by sentence functions that are satisfied in every world that differs from this world at most only with respect to its initial conditions:

A statement may be said to be naturally or physically necessary if, and only if, it is deducible from a statement function which is satisfied in all worlds that differ from our world, if at all, only with respect to initial conditions. (Popper 1965, p. 433)

A statement function is an expression, such as "$Rxt \rightarrow Axt$", which can be converted into a sentence that is true or is false by any of several alternative methods. One of these, for example, involves prefixing appropriate quantifiers to produce a universal generalization of form (UG-1).

What Popper is suggesting is that there is a fundamental difference between natural necessities and universal generalizations of this kind. A fair approximation of his position could be conveyed by saying that natural necessities are true of all physically possible worlds, while universal generalizations are not, where physically possible worlds can be understood as possible histories that this world might have undergone, were its "initial conditions" subject to arbitrary variations. Since there is only one actual history of the world, we could easily confound them.

If the reference properties and attributes that are the objects of lawful relations have to be universals, then that would suggest an alternative solution to Goodman's Paradox. *Universals* should be understood as properties that, in principle, can be attributed to (or "predicated" of) any member of any possible world (Fetzer 1981, p. 191). By virtue of their explicit definition by means of a temporal reference that uniquely refers to some particular moment t in the history of the actual world, however, "grue" and "bleen," unlike "blue" and "green," are not predicates of kinds that are predicable of any member of any possible world except this one.

The identification of universals with dispositions takes the problem another step forward. If we assume that *dispositions* are tendencies to display specific responses under suitable conditions, then (pure) *gold* and *malleability* would appear to be suitable candidates to function as reference properties and as attributes in lawlike sentences. If such an account could be sustained, then the truth of at least some subjunctive and counterfactual conditionals might be explained as manifestations of underlying dispositions. On initial consideration, this would appear to provide an ontological and semantical solution for part of the problem.

Perhaps the reason why hypothesis $h1$, *everything gold is malleable*, seems to be law might also be because, in any such physically possible world, everything that is gold would be malleable. And the reason why hypothesis $h2$, *all my friends are rich*, does not seem to be a law might also be because it is not the case that, in any such physically possible world, all my friends would be rich. Of course, in those worlds in which I and my friends do not exist, hypothesis $h2$ turns out to be trivially true, because everything would be such that either it is not my friend or it is rich. But, in those possible worlds in which I and my friends do exist, in some worlds they would be rich but in other worlds they would not.

Popper's approach is extremely suggestive, but it encounters several problems. His formulation, like Goodman's thesis (T1), does not differentiate logical truths from nonlogical truths, since every sentence function that is true on grammatical on vocabulary grounds alone can satisfy both of their conceptions. For example, Popper contrasts material conditionals of the form '$a \rightarrow b$' with natural necessities of the form '$N(a \rightarrow b)$' thus:

(A) '$N(a \rightarrow b)$' is not always true if a is false in contradistinction to '$a \rightarrow b$';
(B) '$N(a \rightarrow b)$' is not always true if b is true, in contradistinction to '$a \rightarrow b$';
(C) '$N(a \rightarrow b)$' is always true if a is necessarily false (whether by logical or by physical necessity); and,
(D) '$N(a \rightarrow b)$' is always true if b is necessarily true (whether by logical or by physical necessity). (Popper 1965, p. 434)

And he suggests that these principles may be those that define what other authors have taken to be the "subjunctive" or "counterfactual" conditional.

Popper's conditions (A) and (B) differentiate logical and physical necessities from material conditionals, but his conditions (C) and (D) do not differentiate physical necessities from logical necessities. This problem does not appear to be too difficult to resolve, since they can be revised:

(C′)   '$N(a \rightarrow b)$' is never true if a is logically impossible in contradistinction to '$\square(a \rightarrow b)$'; and,
(D′)   '$N(a \rightarrow b)$' is never true if b is logically necessary in contradistinction to '$\square(a \rightarrow b)$'. (Fetzer 1981, p. 195)

Physical necessities, after all, unlike logical necessities, should *never* be true whenever either their antecedents are logically impossible or their consequents are logically necessary. This appears to qualify as genuine progress, but a far more serious obstacle confronts this account of laws.

PERMANENT PROPERTIES

While Popper's conception of natural necessity appears to be flawed, an alternative conception of permanent properties supports Popper's approach without begging the question by supplying an ontological foundation that may contribute to understanding the nature of laws.

Suppose we pursue Popper's suggestion that natural necessity may be rather similar to the conception of subjunctive conditionality that others have considered. If we accept the principle that subjunctive conditionals imply corresponding material conditionals, as the following thesis claims,

(GP-2) If '. . . $\gg$ _____', then '. . . $\rightarrow$ _____',

and, contrary to Popper, maintain the principle that any lawlike sentence must be nonanalytic, then the following relationships appear to be true:

(UG-6) If '$(x)(t)(Rxt \gg Axt)$' is a law, then '$(x)(t)(Rxt \rightarrow Axt)$' and
     it is not the case that '$\Box(x)(t)(Rxt \rightarrow Axt)$'.

As in the case of (UG-5), the problem remains of discovering the precise conditions under which a sentence with a certain logical form is a law.

We have discovered that Goodman offers a solution to the question, "When are we entitled to regard a sentence as lawlike?", which could be expressed in the following fashion: "We are entitled to regard a sentence of the form, '$(x)(t)(Rxt \rightarrow Axt)$', as a law when and only when several specific conditions are satisfied in relation to an epistemic context, including that '$(x)(t)(Rxt \rightarrow Axt)$' is supported, unviolated, and unexhausted." Whatever its merits may turn out to be as an answer to this question, it does not provide an answer to the question, "What does it mean for a sentence to be lawlike?" Goodman addresses the wrong question.

Popper at least considers the right question, "What does it mean for a sentence to be lawlike?", but his answer appears to be unacceptable for an equally serious reason, namely: the definition of physical or natural necessity seems to presuppose the very notion that it is intended to explain. But if this is indeed the case, then it is circular and does not provide more than a partial solution to the problem that needs to be solved. Thus, while Popper wants to use the class of worlds that differ from this one "only with respect to initial conditions," this feat of mental subtraction may or may not yield the intended membership in the class of laws.

Suppose, for example, that a Humean analysis were adopted, so laws *are* merely constant conjunctions or relative frequencies that happen to obtain during the history of this world. Were the initial conditions that initiate the history of this world subject to change, the constant conjunctions and relative frequencies that obtained during this world's history might have been entirely different. The set of statement functions that are satisfied by every world that differs from this world, if at all, only with respect to its initial conditions might turn out to be an empty set.

Popper's conception is intuitively enticing, but it cannot provide an adequate explication of natural laws unless it can explain which worlds are possible and why. Nevertheless, a Popperian solution might yet be possible by building upon Popper's emphasis on the character of laws as *structural properties that have the force of prohibitions* (Popper 1965, p. 428). The conception of laws as prohibitions on possible worlds, moreover, harmonizes well with the traditional conception of laws as regularities that cannot be violated and cannot be changed. And it hints that lawlike hypotheses might be tested by attempting to refute them.

Indeed, a suitable solution to the problem of law appears to require a fundamental distinction between "permanent" and "transient" properties, where *permanent properties* are contingent dispositions that something cannot lose without also losing a corresponding reference property. Thus, in relation to a language **L,** *an attribute A is a permanent property of everything that has a reference property R just in case there is no process or procedure, natural or contrived, by means of which a thing could lose attribute A without also losing the reference property R,* where the possession of A by something that is R must be logically contingent in **L** (Fetzer 1981, pp. 38–39). These conditions are essential to natural laws.

There appear to be three different ways in which a specific thing can possess a certain property. The first occurs whenever the attribute A is a property of every instance of reference property R as a function of our language. These are properties that things of a certain kind possess as a matter of definition. The second occurs whenever attribute A is something that one or more instances of property R happens to have as a transient attribute. These are properties these things could lose while still remaining of kind R. The third occurs whenever attribute A is something that every instance of property R must have because A is a permanent property of R. These are the properties that provide a foundation for understanding laws.

We know that any bachelor has to be unmarried, for example, because (being) *unmarried* is part of what it means to be a "bachelor." It would be logically impossible for something that is a bachelor to be married (for something that is a rose to not be a *flower*, and so on) unless our language were to change. Even if every Corvette ever manufactured happens to be painted *red* (or every No. 2 pencil were *made in the USA*, and so forth), we know that these properties are ones that Corvettes and pencils could lose while remaining things of that kind. A Corvette could be repainted *blue*, but it would still be a Corvette. A pencil could be *made in China* and still be suitable for writing. These are not properties those things have by law.

The difference between hypothesis $h1$, *everything gold is malleable*, and hypothesis $h2$, *all my friends are rich*, should now be fairly obvious. When "gold" is defined in terms of atomic number, it turns out that things that are gold have the same melting point, the same boiling point, and the same specific gravity as properties they could lose only by no longer being things that are gold. Other properties, including the shape, size, and selling price of things that are gold are attributes that things that are gold could gain or lose while still remaining things that are gold. The price of a gold coin may go up or may go down, but that does not change its metal.

The problem of distinguishing between lawful and accidental generalizations thus arises because every member of a reference class could have the same transient property in common. Even if all my friends happen to be rich, that does not mean they could not lose their shirts in the market tomorrow! But they could remain my friends, as always. The underlying explanation for the existence of a lawful relationship between property R and attribute A is that A happens to be a permanent property of R, where:

(GP-3) If A is a *permanent property* of R, then '$(x)(t)(Rxt \Rrightarrow Axt)$'.

Thus, permanent properties provide an ontic justification for subjunctives.

Since we have discovered that analytic relations imply corresponding subjunctive conditionals, as (GP-1) asserts, evidently subjunctives can be justified on logical or on ontological grounds. On the assumption that the *only* modes of justification for subjunctives are logical and ontological, it would be possible to formalize these relationships by the following claim:

(UG-7) If '$(x)(t)(Rxt \Rrightarrow Axt)$' and it is not the case that '$\Box(x)(t)(Rxt \to Axt)$', then '$(x)(t)(Rxt \Rrightarrow Axt)$' is a law.

Whether or not this assumption is ultimately justifiable is a matter that we shall consider in the chapters that follow. But it appears to be true.

If these reflections are well-founded, then a solution to the problem of law may be at hand. The approach that I am recommending is weaker than the Aristotelian conception, because it does not commit us to the metaphysics of essential properties. But this result is welcome, because Aristotle's conception was too strong. It is also stronger than the Humean conception, because it permits us to draw an ontological distinction between genuine laws and accidental generalizations. The difference is not merely a question of attitude or a matter of subjective expectation. This result is also welcome, because Hume's conception was too weak.

The conception of permanent properties as the foundation for laws supplies an appropriate answer to the question, "What does it mean for a sentence to be lawlike?", which goes well beyond Goodman's preoccupation with the question, "When are we entitled to regard a sentence as lawlike?" And it also goes beyond Popper's conception of natural necessities as those that are described by sentence functions that are satisfied in every world that differs from this world, if at all, only with respect to its initial conditions. Its consequences for understanding conditionals of different kinds support Popper's theses (A) and (B) but also (C') and (D').

Whether this approach can provide an adequate explication of the nature of laws is a matter that we shall have to consider. Even though we have located a solution that is weaker than Aristotle's and stronger than Hume's, it might still be too strong or too weak. And we have to ascertain whether it can satisfy appropriate epistemic conditions. Nevertheless, an ontological and semantical solution of this kind seems to explain not only why some generalizations but not others provide support for subjunctives and counterfactuals but also why methods that are appropriate for establishing mere generalizations may not be suitable for the discovery of laws.

The conception of permanent properties provides a basis for viewing lawlike sentences as logically contingent subjunctive conditionals. It is weaker than Aristotle's conception and stronger than Hume's. But its adequacy depends on epistemic questions that remain unexplored.

CHAPTER THREE

WHAT ARE SCIENTIFIC THEORIES?

onsideration of the difficulties involved in defining dispositional predicates indicates that both the standard conception of scientific theories and its semantic alternative have serious deficiencies. The problem of provisoes suggests that theories are often envisioned as idealizations.

THE STANDARD CONCEPTION

Logical empiricism endorsed the conception of a scientific theory as an abstract calculus combined with an empirical interpretation. By embracing a distinction between observational and theoretical predicates, it differentiated between empirical laws and theoretical laws.

If there is an alternative to the conception of the aim of science as that of discovering laws of nature, it must be that science aims at the discovery of scientific theories. Indeed, the most prevalent view would be that laws can be invoked to explain and predict the occurrence of particular events during the course of the world's history, while theories in turn may be invoked to explain those laws themselves. Alternatively, a distinction may be drawn between laws of different kinds, where theories consist of theoretical laws, but other laws may be merely empirical. On either approach, however, theories and laws are closely related, if not the very same thing.

Carnap supplies a conception that combines the features of both alternatives (Carnap 1966, pp. 225–246). Drawing a distinction between the observational and the nonobservational elements of the vocabulary of a theory, he suggests that *theoretical laws* are general-izations whose nonlogical terms are exclusively theoretical and that *empirical laws* are generalizations whose nonlogical terms are exclu-sively observational. A *scientific theory* consists of theoretical laws and correspondence rules, which relate theoretical laws to observable phenomena by employing a mixed nonlogical vocabulary. An empiri-cal law might be explained by its derivation from a theory.

Carnap maintains that the distinction between the observational and the nonobservational elements of the vocabulary of a theory can be drawn two different ways. Philosophers tend to adopt a narrower sense, according to which a predicate is *observational* only if the presence or the absence of a designated property can be ascertained on the basis of direct observation. Scientists, however, tend to adopt a broader sense, according to which predicates are *observational* when the presence or the absence of such properties can be ascertained on the basis of direct observation or relatively simple measurement. No decisive reasons favor one over the other approach.

Empirical laws (such as "All swans are white") pose no special epistemic problems, since they can be discovered by means of simple inductive procedures. If m/n observed swans have been white, for example, then when an appropriate number have been observed over an appropriate range of conditions, infer (inductively) that m/n swans are white (or, when $m = n$, that all swans are white). A somewhat similar rule, which Brian Skyrms calls "*Rule S*," avoids generaliza-tions in making predictions (Skyrms 1975). According to S, if m/n observed swans have been white, then the degree of support for the inductive inference that the next swan will be white $= m/n$.

Theoretical laws (such as those of genetics), however, may not be established by simple inductive procedures. The approach most ap-propriate to their discovery is *the hypothetico-deductive method*, according to which a theoretical hypothesis can be subjected to empirical test by deriving consequences couched in observational language. If certain hypotheses concerning the laws of genetics imply that, within suitable populations, the distribution of a specific trait (such as epilepsy, blue eyes, and so on) should assume the average relative frequency of m/n, those theoretical hypotheses can be indirectly tested within those populations when those traits are observable.

This conception presumes that members of the target population can be identified on the basis of suitable empirical tests. If the target population were Scandinavians, then access to evidence that a person were a Dane or a Norwegian or a Swede or an Icelander would be required. Merely claiming to be a Swede, for example, provides no guarantee that a person is Swedish, but the possession of relevant documents, such as a Swedish passport and a Swedish birth certificate, and fluency in Swedish might be sufficient to classify a person as Swedish rather than, say, as an impostor working for the CIA.

Although Carnap supports the conception of scientific theories as sets of theoretical laws and correspondence rules, he also endorses a more formal explication according to which *a scientific theory consists of an abstract calculus coupled with an empirical interpretation.* An abstract calculus, say,

1. $(x)(t)(Wxt \rightarrow Xxt)$ Axiom
2. $(x)(t)[Xxt \rightarrow (Yxt \rightarrow Zxt)]$ Axiom
3. $(x)(t)[Wxt \rightarrow (Yxt \rightarrow Zxt)]$ Theorem

Figure 2. An Abstract Calculus

where "W," "X," "Y," and "Z" are predicate variables and "_____ $\rightarrow$ . . ." is the material conditional sign, provides a theory schema that can be converted into a theory by supplying an empirical interpretation. "W" and "X," for example, might be replaced by theoretical predicates and "Y" and "Z" by observational.

As an illustration, Carnap discusses the distinction between uninterpreted and interpreted axiom systems within geometry. Although it is possible to study formal systems as sets of axioms and deduce theorems that follow from them, it is also possible to provide them with an empirical interpretation whereby those axioms become theoretical hypotheses and those theorems empirically testable. By interpreting lines as paths of light rays and points as their intersections, Euclidean geometry can be converted from a domain of pure mathematics into one of applied mathematics, where previously purely formal claims assume the character of empirical hypotheses.

A different illustration might involve *intelligence* (or "IQ") as it has often been envisioned. A modest theory of intelligence might maintain that there are various levels of general intelligence (say, high, average, and low) that influence human behavior, where a person's level of intelligence can, under suitable conditions, be measured by his performance on specially designed tests called "IQ tests." Thus, although a person's intelligence level qualifies as a theoretical property that cannot be directly observed, levels of intelligence might still be measured indirectly by an IQ test as a function of the number of questions answered correctly, which, multiplied by a scale constant, yields a mental age that, if divided by a person's age, equals his "IQ."

Thus, a test of 200 weighted questions might represent possible scores from 0 to 10000, where a person aged 25 who scored 3800 would have an IQ equal to 152. That person would then be classified as possessing high intelligence, if the range of scores for various classifications ran more or less as follows: 0 to 70 = low; 71 to 129 = average; 130 to 200 = high. Precisely which questions should be asked and which answers should be counted as correct as well as the appropriate ranges for various classifications would have to be decided by those who design and conduct these tests, partially as a function of the distribution of scores within the target population and partially as a function of the purpose that this test is intended to achieve.

Assuming the members of the target group *TG* can be identified using suitable criteria, the hypothesis that the members of that population have IQs within a certain range (high, for example) would mean that, if the members of that population were subjected to an IQ test, their IQ scores would fall between 130 and 200. This approach could be formalized as follows:

1. $(x)(t)(TGxt \rightarrow IQxt = high)$ Hypothesis
2. $\Box(x)(t)[IQxt = high \rightarrow (TTxt \rightarrow TSxt = 130\ to\ 200)]$ Definition
3. $(x)(t)[TGxt \rightarrow (TTxt \rightarrow TSxt = 130\ to\ 200)]$ Theorem

Figure 3. A Specific Instance

where Figure 3 is a specific instance of Figure 2. These sentences, informally expressed, assert respectively, "Every member of *TG* has a high IQ," "Everyone with a high IQ obtains a score falling between 130 and 200 if they take an IQ test," and "Every member of *TG* obtains a score falling between 130 and 200 if they take an IQ test," where the first is the hypothesis, the second is a truth by definition, and the third follows from them. According to Carnap's conception—which is known as *the standard conception*—a theory of this variety would properly qualify as a scientific theory.

THE ANALYTIC AND THE SYNTHETIC (AGAIN)

The standard conception provides a solution to the epistemological problems involved in subjecting theories to empirical tests. But it presupposes an observational/theoretical distinction that appears problematic in relation to the definition of dispositional predicates.

The most striking feature of the standard conception is that it affords a possible solution to the epistemic problems represented by theory squares. A theory square corresponding to this theory would look like the following:

Property [*TG*] is related by law to attribute [*IQ*]

deductively		deductively
or		or
inductively		inductively

Empirical test for [*TG*] is correlated with empirical test for [*IQ*]

Figure 4. A Theory Square

Thus, sentence 1 is a theoretical hypothesis, sentence 2 an analytic truth, and sentence 3 an empirical generalization that follows from them. If the correlation between the results of tests for *TG* and for *IQ* did not bear an appropriate correspondence to the hypothesis, it would be disconfirmed. Thus, the combination of the analytic/synthetic distinction with the observational/theoretical distinction affords what appears to be a very promising approach to the epistemic problems encountered by scientific theories.

Nevertheless, the standard conception confronts major obstacles. One is the tenability of the distinction between observational and theoretical predicates, which has been attacked by Frederick Suppe, among others (Suppe 1972). Distinguishing between predicates and properties, Suppe suggests that sometimes *observational predicates* do not designate observable properties and that sometimes *theoretical predicates* do designate observable properties. When a blue object is shattered into minute pieces, it may no longer be possible to observe their blueness; and when I insert my thumb into a socket, I may observe an electric current. If this is the case, however, then the alleged distinction between them seems rather obscure.

Another, of course, is the defensibility of extensional language for the formalization of scientific theories. In Chapter Two it was proposed that the difference between accidental and lawlike generalizations may be accounted for on the basis of the permanent/transient property distinction, where permanent property relations between R and A can be formalized by means of logically contingent subjunctive generalizations. But if that is the case, we ought to expect that the standard conception will confront exactly the same difficulties. Indeed, these problems are related and represent one of the main difficulties that the logical empiricist program was never able to successfully resolve, namely: *the problem of defining dispositional predicates*.

The distinction between observational and theoretical predicates was often drawn as Carnap has drawn it, but sometimes a further distinction was drawn between "observational," "dispositional," and "theoretical" predicates, where a predicate is *dispositional* when it designates a tendency to display specific response behavior under suitable test conditions. Even predicates that initially appear to be observable, such as "blue," and predicates that initially appear to be theoretical, such as "electric current," might turn out to be tendencies to display various response behaviors under appropriate test conditions. The challenge confronted by the logical empiricists was to discover a way to define dispositional predicates using extensional logic.

The general conception of *intelligence* under consideration here represents an approach of this kind. Suppose, for example, that sentence 2 of Figure 3 were rewritten here as a definition of the meaning of "high IQ":

(D1) x has a high IQ at t =df if x takes an IQ test at t, then x obtains a score that is between 130 and 200 at t.

Thus, assuming that "x takes an IQ test at t" and "x obtains a score that is between 130 and 200 at t" are both observational predicates whose satisfaction or not can be ascertained in any specific case on the basis of direct observation or relatively simple measurement, perhaps this term might be completely definable by means of extensional logic and observables alone.

The problem, however, is that the definiens, as a material conditional, has the same meaning as "either it is not the case that x takes an IQ test at t or x obtains a score that is between 130 and 200 at t." This means that anything trivially satisfies this definition at any time it is not subjected to the specified test condition. So a yellow cow (a leather sofa, and so forth) has a *high IQ* so long as it does not take a test of this kind. Moreover, the situation is even worse on the assumption that "low IQ" and "average IQ" are similarly defined, because then anything trivially satisfies them all at any time it is not subjected to the specified test condition, which means a yellow cow (a leather sofa, and so on) has an *average* and a *low IQ* as well.

Such a situation was obviously intolerable. Carnap proposed a method that might preserve the use of extensional logic and observational language for this purpose through the use of forms known as *reduction sentences*, which specify the meaning of a predicate in relation to the test condition (Carnap 1936–37). Some reduction sentences were known as "unilateral":

(D2)   if x takes an IQ test at t, then if x obtains a score that is
        between 130 and 200 at t, then x has a high IQ at t; or,

(D3)   if x takes an IQ test at t, then if x has a high IQ at t, then
        x obtains a score that is between 130 and 200 at t.

Thus, according to (D2), if Johnny Jones takes an IQ test, then obtaining a score between 130 and 200 is a sufficient condition for him to have a high IQ. And, according to (D3), if he takes an IQ test, then having a high IQ is a sufficient condition for Johnny to obtain a score between 130 and 200.

This approach improved upon the method of explicit definition that is represented by (D1), because anything that does not take an IQ test does not trivially satisfy the definiens. A price was being paid, however, since it meant that the notion of "IQ" had no meaning for those who never took the test. Reduction sentences thus provided only partial rather than complete definitions of the meaning of predicates. Moreover, the restriction to observable test conditions had the uningratiating consequence of prohibiting any consideration of unobservable properties that might affect an individual's performance. According to (D2), for example, if Johnny obtained the score of 33 on the test, then that was his IQ, even if he had had severe stress during the test after staying up all night worrying about it.

Carnap also introduced a further variation on the same theme in the form of "bilateral" reduction sentences, which combine (D2) with (D3):

(D4)   if x takes an IQ test at t, then x obtains a score that is
        between 130 and 200 at t if and only if x has a high IQ at t.

This meant that obtaining a score between 130 and 200 on an IQ test is both necessary and sufficient for having a high IQ for those who take it. However, there could be more than one bilateral reduction sentence for each predicate. Suppose that anyone with a high IQ would also have the ability to always make correct change when they work as a cashier:

(D5)   if *x* works as a cashier at *t*, then *x* has a high IQ at *t* if and only if *x* always makes correct change at *t*.

But the conjunction of (D4) with (D5) implies that anyone who scores between 130 and 200 on an IQ test who works as a cashier always makes correct change. This was a most unwelcome result, because it meant that two reduction sentences that were supposed to be *analytic* could have deductive consequences that were *synthetic* (Hempel 1965, pp. 114–115).

THE DOGMA OF REDUCTIONISM

The attempt to reduce the meaning of dispositional predicates to material conditionals with test conditions and outcome responses expressed by means of observational predicates cannot be sustained, which lends support to Quine's rejection of the second of his dogmas of empiricism.

You may recall that, in Chapter One, I mentioned that Quine also criticizes what he called "the dogma of reductionism." This dogma consists of the belief that "each meaningful statement is equivalent to some logical construct upon terms that refer to immediate experience" (Quine 1953, p. 20). Our review of the logical empiricists' efforts to define dispositional predicates reflects a commitment to this conception. (D1) through (D4) represent successively more and more sophisticated efforts to specify the meaning of a dispositional predicate while relying exclusively upon the resources of observational predicates and extensional logic. These efforts yielded the disturbing finding that analytic sentences could have synthetic consequences.

Hempel recognized that these problems were manifestations of the use of the material conditional and admitted that subjunctive conditionals might be thought to provide a possible solution. But Goodman's work and that of others suggested to him that that approach confronted problems of its own (Hempel 1965, p. 109). Moreover, although his contribution to the issue is not generally acknowledged, Popper provided powerful arguments that the observational/theoretical distinction could not be sustained because observational and theoretical *properties* are properly understood as *dispositions*.

Popper's position was especially persuasive because he argued in terms of very familiar examples. Thus, he maintained that the use of universals such as "glass" or "water," in sentences like, "Here is a glass of water," necessarily transcend experience, because in describing something as *glass* or as *water*, we are attributing to it innumerable tendencies to behave in innumerable different ways under various test conditions. Because *all universals are dispositions* in this sense, none of them can be reduced to or defined by observational predicates and extensional logic, as Carnap attempted. Thus,

In general, the dispositional character of any universal property will become clear if we consider what tests we should undertake if we are in doubt whether or not the property is present in some particular case . . . [T]he attempt to distinguish between dispositional and non-dispositional predicates is mistaken, just as is the attempt to distinguish between theoretical terms (or languages) and non-theoretical or empirical or observational or factual or ordinary terms (or languages). (Popper 1965, p. 425)

Indeed, subjunctives and counterfactuals would be required to unpack the meaning of universals of either the "observational" or the "theoretical" kind.

Even Suppe's examples could be understood as diverse manifestations of underlying dispositions. Something blue might look purple under red lights or look black when the lights are out. An electric current might move the needle of an ammeter as it flows through a circuit, but not when the equipment is broken. When a blue object is shattered into minute pieces, it may no longer be possible to observe its blueness, unless enough of those pieces could be glued together again. And when I insert my thumb into a socket, I may observe an electric current, but not if I were wearing rubber gloves. These properties, properly understood, turn out to be dispositional in kind.

But this meant that logical empiricism confronted a dilemma at precisely this juncture. The analytic/synthetic distinction, the observational/theoretical distinction, and a methodological commitment to extensional logic define the movement. But it now became apparent that the analytic/synthetic distinction could be sustained only at the expense of the methodological commitment to extensional logic. The methodological commitment to extensional logic could be sustained only at the expense of the analytic/synthetic distinction. Even the observational/theoretical distinction could not be justified in its traditional guise if all universals were dispositional, as Popper claimed.

As a consequence, Carnap and Hempel would become penetrating critics of their own doctrines: Hempel, for example, as one of the foremost skeptics concerning the analytic/synthetic distinction; Carnap, as one of the foremost proponents of intensional language frameworks. In years following, Hempel would emerge as a major opponent of naive views regarding the observational/theoretical distinction (Hempel 1970). He would subsequently elaborate the view that dispositional explanation is of a kind with theoretical (Hempel 1977). As a consequence, the leading members of logical empiricism itself would demonstrate that logical empiricism could not be sustained.

From the intensional point of view, no doubt, it would be more appropriate to maintain that theoretical explanations are "of a kind" with dispositional, since there appears to be no justification for the assumption that observational and theoretical predicates designate other-than-dispositional properties: *the kind of property dispositions are does not depend upon the ease with which their presence or absence may be ascertained on the basis of experiential findings alone*. As Carnap himself would lucidly maintain:

Once the problem of the explication of nomic form has been solved and a logic of causal modalities has been constructed, it will be possible to use these modalities for the explication of subjunctive and, in particular, of counter-factual conditionals. Presumably, it will then also be possible to introduce disposition terms by explicit definition. (Carnap 1963, p. 952)

Indeed, the manner in which the difficulties that we have found in defining "intelligence" might be solved exemplifies the significance of this view.

Let us assume that "$IQxt = high$" means that x has a high IQ at t,

"*TTxt*" that *x* takes an IQ test at *t*, and "*TSxt* = *130 to 200*" that *x*'s test score falls between 130 and 200 at *t*," as before. Then (D1) might be formalized as:

(D6) $IQxt = high =$df $TTxt \rightarrow TSxt = 130$ *to* $200.$

But, since the definiens means the same thing as "either it is not the case that *x* takes an IQ test at *t* or *x*'s test score falls between 130 and 200 at *t*," we have discovered that anything trivially satisfies the definiens at any time it is not subjected to the specified test condition. To avoid the problem of yellow cows (leather sofas, and so on) as things of high intelligence, the material conditional should be replaced by its subjunctive counterpart.

Thus, by employing the subjunctive instead of the material conditional, the problem of trivial satisfiability of the definiens appears to be avoided:

(D7) $IQxt = high =$df $TTxt \gg TSxt = 130$ *to* $200.$

For this definition asserts that *x* has a high IQ at *t* just in case if *x* were to take an IQ test at *t*, then *x* would obtain a test score between 130 to 200, which assumes the satisfaction—hypothetically or otherwise—of that test condition. No one, presumably, would want to maintain that yellow cows (leather sofas, and the like) qualify as highly intelligent things given (D7). Nevertheless, there are reasons to doubt that even (D7) itself is adequate.

Surely there are situations in which our performance on a test is not an accurate indication of our aptitude, abilities, or attainments. Suppose that Johnny subsequently retook the test after a good night's rest and obtained a score of 110. It would be ridiculous to maintain he had actually gained 77 IQ points in the meanwhile! This case suggests that there may be many other factors $F1, F2, \ldots, Fn$—such as whether we are emotionally upset (physically impaired, and so on)—that might influence our score but do not change our intelligence. Such factors have to be taken into account.

When the presence or the absence of other factors in addition to taking the test is taken into account, we obtain an even more adequate definition:

(D8) $IQxt = high =$ df $(TTxt \& F1xt \& \ldots \& Fnxt) \Rightarrow TSxt = 130 \text{ to } 200.$

Yet while (D8) appears to be moving in the right direction, unobservable factors $Fixt$—such as whether or not x is feeling apathetic (high on grass, and so forth)—could be excluded only by forfeiting its significance. Thus, an adequate definition of a property of this kind dictates abandoning the methodological commitment to extensional logic and the attempt to define dispositional predicates by means of mere observational predicates alone. Yet even the subjunctive conditional turns out to be too weak for this role.

THE SEMANTIC CONCEPTION

Motivated by disenchantment with the standard conception (largely due to the untenability of the observational/theoretical distinction, on the one hand, and the intractability of the problem of law, on the other), the semantic conception has been advanced as an alternative.

When Quine questioned the dogma of reductionism, when Goodman displayed the limitations of extensional logic, and when Popper challenged the observational/theoretical distinction, each of them thereby contributed to depriving the logical empiricist program of its plausibility. Even though most students agree that logical empiricism can no longer be defended in its classic guise, however, none of the views offered as alternatives has been very successful in taking its place. One approach has been to abandon the observational/theoretical distinction while retaining the analytic/synthetic distinction by adopting an alternative account of scientific theories, now known as "the semantic conception."

In place of the standard conception, Patrick Suppes, Joseph Sneed, and Frederick Suppe, among others, building on the prior work of

E. W. Beth, advanced *the semantic conception*, where theories are envisioned as set-theoretical predicates, as state-spaces, or as relational structures (Suppe 1989, p. 4). In its simplest versions, scientific theories consist of *theoretical definitions* that define theoretical predicates, where *empirical hypotheses* might relate those predicates to specific portions of the world. Theoretical definitions and empirical hypotheses thus displace the theoretical laws and the correspondence rules that were the standard conception.

Ronald Giere, for example, has suggested that theoretical predicates can define different kinds of systems (Giere 1979). A *classical particle system* might be defined as a system that obeys Newton's three laws of motion and the inverse-square law of universal gravitation. The empirical hypothesis could then be asserted that the Sun and planets of our solar system constitute a classical particle system. As Suppe has observed, these theories are characteristically supposed to possess counterfactual import, because the systems to which they apply satisfy conditions that are idealized, such as being subject exclusively to gravitational forces (Suppe 1989, pp. 153–54).

It ought to be observed, however, that, although Suppe acknowledges that support for counterfactual conditionals is an accepted requirement of natural laws, the kind of *counterfactual idealization* Suppe has in mind for scientific theories is of a decidedly different kind. On this approach, theories describe *the behavior that a system would exhibit were it the case that such a system satisfied the conditions specified by the theory*. The counterfactual significance of a theory is not to be found in the content of its laws but rather in whatever distinguishes that theory from the world. He even denies that laws themselves need to possess counterfactual force.

The counterfactual significance of theories on this account is located instead "in the relation between the idealized system described by the laws and the actual typically nonidealized circumstances obtaining in the world" (Suppe 1989, p. 166). What this reveals is that the semantic conception offers no analysis of the truth conditions for lawlike sentences. No attention is devoted to the kind of relationship obtaining between a reference predicate R and an attribute A when that relation is lawlike, and no consideration is given to the kinds of predicates that can occur as reference and attribute predicates. No subjunctive conditionals appear in its laws.

This is clearly a feature of the semantic conception. While some definitions might stipulate that certain laws must be satisfied by systems of the kind that they define, these laws may or may not have the characteristics of natural laws. A *normal driving system* could be defined as a system of drivers, automobiles, and highways that satisfies the valid-license law, the 65 mph speed-limit law, and the unexpired-auto-tag law. The empirical claim might then be made that Minnesota is a normal driving system. But even if this were true, it would completely fail to distinguish between laws of nature and laws of society or between genuine laws and merely accidental generalizations, a difficulty also confronted by the standard conception.

If theories *are* counterfactual idealizations, then it would appear to be a relevant question to ask how they are related to the actual behavior of phenomena in the physical world. Suppe claims that "auxiliary theories" should be "used to determine how the actual situation will deviate from the idealized situation," thereby yielding accurate predictions of actual behavior. If auxiliary theories of this kind are possible, however, then *less* counterfactual and *less* idealized theories are obtainable, whose discovery would seem to be an altogether more appropriate aim of scientific inquiry.

If auxiliary theories are *not* possible, of course, the point of theories is obscure. Suppe distinguishes theories that incorporate laws of succession, laws of coexistence, and laws of interaction, which impose limits upon the behavior of physical systems. The kind of limitation involved here, however, is definitional: systems that do not obey these "laws" are simply not systems of that kind. A theory is said to be *true* when the class of "theory-induced" physical systems is identical with the class of "causally possible" physical systems, where the latter are phenomena in the world. But this hints that theories might be viewed as sets of lawlike sentences instead.

The conception of theories as sets of laws that apply within a common domain, after all, provides a more elegant account, even if it has to be supplemented by "dictionary definitions," which might be partial or complete. Moreover, Suppe emphasizes that the semantic conception dispenses with the correspondence rules required by the standard conception. But without some counterpart to explain the relationship between theories and evidence, his own account could not be sustained. Even the theory-ladenness of observational language does not show that observational language is "theory laden" in specific respects that undermine its utility for testing theories.

One of the fascinating features of the semantic conception is the extent to which its adherents tend to disagree on fundamental aspects of theories. Although Suppe himself abandons the observational/theoretical distinction, Bas van Fraassen retains it. While Suppe supposes that laws are invariable elements of scientific theories, van Fraassen rejects them. And while Suppe is a special kind of realist, van Fraassen is best viewed as a neo-instrumentalist. Indeed, on van Fraassen's view, but not on Suppe's, there is no more to the adequacy of any theory than its empirical (or "observational") content (van Fraassen 1989). These are issues to which we will return in Chapter Eight.

Since both Suppe and van Fraassen adhere to the semantic conception, it should be obvious that a commitment to laws of nature is not entailed thereby. Indeed, it is difficult to resist the conclusion that the semantic conception is really the standard conception of an abstract calculus that might be supplied various (partial or complete) interpretations, where the notion of satisfaction for predicates has displaced the notion of truth for sentences. Since Alfred Tarski has shown that truth is reducible to satisfaction for formalized structures of most of the kinds that appeal to semantic theorists, the benefits of such an exchange may be difficult to discern. How theories are to satisfy appropriate epistemic constraints that might turn them into empirically testable explanations is especially difficult to understand.

THE PLACE OF PROVISOES

Since the semantic conception envisions scientific theories as counterfactual idealizations whose conditions are seldom if ever satisfied by systems in the world, the scope of applicability of those theories would appear to be severely restricted, generating the problem of provisoes.

From the perspective of a theory square, no doubt, the benefits of the semantic conception by contrast with the standard conception are obscure, indeed. The standard conception wedded the observational/theoretical distinction to the analytic/synthetic distinction and produced the conception of scientific theories as theoretical laws and correspondence rules. While Suppe envisions theories as "abstract structures," even he concedes that they do not become physical theories until they are given "physical interpretations," where these interpretations may be merely "implicitly or intensionally specified and are liable to alteration, modification, or expansion as science progresses" (Suppe 1989, pp. 422–23).

Hempel's study of the inferential role of scientific theories raises yet other difficulties for theories on the semantic conception (Hempel 1988). Suppose we assume that theories *are* properly understood as idealizations of the behavior that would be displayed by physical systems under certain (typically counterfactual) conditions. Then any inferences concerning past or future occurrences would depend upon logically contingent assumptions about the presence or the absence of such conditions. The laws of magnetic attraction, for example, assert that the north and south poles of two metal magnets attract each other, but this does not happen at high temperatures.

Thus, "provisoes" should be envisioned as clauses that pertain to specific applications of a theory that assert that, in those instances, no conditions other than those specified by the theory are present. The consequences of the role of provisoes include (i) that the falsification of a scientific theory is more complex than is commonly assumed, (ii) that programs for the elimination of theoretical terms from scientific theories are illusory, (iii) that the instrumentalist conception of scientific theories as calculating devices appears implausible, and (iv) that the notion of the empirical content of a scientific theory is far more problematic than has usually been supposed.

The inferential situation that Hempel has in mind can be schematized abstractly by assuming that a scientific theory consists of sentences with the form of ('if . . . then _____') conditionals of some appropriate kind and that the satisfaction of their antecedent ('. . .') clauses implies the satisfaction of their consequent ('_____') clauses.

The discovery of instances in which those antecedents (or "initial conditions") were satisfied but those consequents were not, ordinarily would be taken to falsify (or, at least, to "disconfirm") such a theory. However, if, by hypothesis, those conditionals have ranges of application that are restricted, then they can be subjected to empirical test only when those very provisoes are satisfied.

These considerations reinforce the importance of auxiliary theories within the context of the semantic conception. But the consequences of the problem of provisoes are at least equally damaging for the standard conception, which is constructed on the basis of the observational/theoretical language distinction. Notice, in particular, that the specific conditions whose presence or absence must be certified by implicit or explicit provisoes are not restricted to exclusively *observable* properties. Thus, in order to test a theory expressed in theoretical and observational predicates, the presence or absence of yet other *theoretical* properties beyond those occurring in the theory may also have to be empirically ascertained.

In view of Hempel's findings, at least two responses are available. One is to infer that scientific theories are only able to provide "explanations" or "predictions" of the behavior of actual things when they happen to display that behavior under ideal conditions. For any other conditions, those theories are, at best, mere approximations. The other is to infer that, in order to provide genuine explanations and predictions of the behavior of actual things, scientific theories must go beyond idealized conditions by taking into account every factor whose presence or absence makes a difference within that domain. As an ideal of science, mere approximation is not enough.

Since lawlike sentences are those that are laws when they are true, the truth of a lawlike sentence implies that such a law takes into account the presence or absence of every property whose presence or absence makes a difference to the occurrence of its attribute. The precise significance of a *requirement of maximal specificity* of this kind, however, depends upon the specific conditions that must be satisfied for the presence or absence of a property to "make a difference" to an attribute. Thus, in the chapter that follows, I shall suggest that lawlike sentences are true only when they are maximally specific on the basis of dispositional (or "causal") criteria of relevance, but other theories of relevance will also be considered.

Before concluding the present chapter, however, several observations may be in order concerning the theory of intelligence that has been used as an example. There appears to be considerable controversy these days over whether there is such a thing as *general intelligence*. There are reasons to suppose human minds may be modular assemblies that consist of differentiated capacities for short-term memory, long-term memory, numerical calculation, facial recognition, and the like. Nevertheless, even if there is no property of general intelligence of the kind under consideration, the same principles of concept formation and theory construction have applicability to other conceptions of aptitudes, abilities, and skills.

Different examples can be drawn from the behavioral sciences, where various kinds of *competence* (mathematical, managerial, linguistic, and so on) are of interest. Whether or not someone is competent at algebra (supervision, English, and so forth) envisioned as a general ability to solve an indefinite number of problems of that kind, for example, is not a directly observable property. It might still be measured indirectly by means of appropriately constructed tests, where those tests could provide usually reliable, but not therefore infallible, evidence as criteria of the presence or the absence of that property. The underlying principles are the same.

Two final points. The use of mathematics is often taken to be an indication of the scientific significance of an hypothesis or theory. Thus, because the theory of intelligence that we have considered here utilizes a measure of *degrees of intelligence* as the foundation for a typology of "high," "average," and "low" levels of intelligence, it might be presumed that this theory is therefore significant. Although concepts tend to fall into qualitative (or "classificatory"), comparative (or "topological"), and quantitative (or "metrical") categories, precise concepts may or may not be important concepts. Empirical testability by itself does not determine theoretical importance. Some precise concepts are actually unimportant.

Hempel, for example, has introduced the concept of a person's "hage," which equals their height in millimeters multiplied by their years of age (Hempel 1952, p. 46). While this property has a quantitative definition, that does not make it theoretically important. What matters (in this and other cases) is the existence of lawful relations between particular reference properties and various attributes. *Hage* is not important because it does not seem to be related by law to any other properties. *Intelligence* is important only provided it is related by law to other human attributes. If there were no more to intelligence than what intelligence tests test, it would not be worth measuring. Scientific significance combines empirical testability with theoretical importance, as we are going to discover again.

If scientific theories are counterfactual idealizations, as the semantic conception asserts, then they must have an extraordinarily limited range of applicability for the purpose of explanation and prediction. The requirement of maximal specificity suggests a possible solution.

CHAPTER FOUR

EXPLICATIONS OF EXPLANATION

The primary benefit from discovering laws of nature is that they can be employed to explain and predict the occurrence of singular events. This chapter surveys the most important explications of explanation: the covering-law, statistical-relevance, and causal-relevance models.

THE COVERING-LAW MODEL

The most influential theory of explanation has been the covering-law model, which combines the conception of explanation by means of subsumption with the conception that explanations are arguments. Some explanations are deductive in form, while others are inductive.

The theory of scientific explanation has been dominated by the conception that explanations for singular events are secured by subsuming them as specific instances of natural laws. During the 1940s, the 1950s, and the 1960s, this approach was systematically elaborated and defended in detail by Carl G. Hempel, who developed what has come to be known as *the covering-law model* of explanation. An essential feature of Hempel's account has been the notion that explanations can always be expressed in the form of arguments, where the premises (called "the explanans") provide grounds, reasons, or evidence supporting the conclusion (called "the explanandum").

Hempel has elaborated the covering-law theory in considerable detail (for example, Hempel 1962 and 1965). Because it has infinitely many relations to other events, no specific event can be explained as a "concrete particular" but only as an event of a certain kind or *under a certain description*. Thus, a distinction must be drawn between an explanandum-phenomenon as a feature of the world's history and an explanandum-sentence as a feature of an explanatory argument. An explanation exhibits the nomic expectability of an explanandum-phenomenon by deriving an explanandum-sentence that describes it from an argument that includes at least one law.

In an early paper, with Paul Oppenheim (Hempel and Oppenheim 1948), Hempel set forth a set of four conditions that were asserted to be necessary and sufficient for an explanandum-phenomenon to be provided with an adequate scientific explanation, which can be formulated in the following way:

(CA-1) the explanandum must be a logical consequence of
        its explanans;
(CA-2) the explanans must include at least one lawlike sentence
        that is actually required for the derivation of the
        explanandum from its explanans;
(CA-3) the explanans must possess empirical content; and,
(CA-4) the explanans must be true.

As Hempel observed, strictly speaking (CA-3) is a redundant requirement, which cannot fail to be satisfied if (CA-1), (CA-2), and (CA-4) are satisfied.

Hempel always realized that these conditions were only appropriate for explanations that appeal to natural laws of universal form, since otherwise the explanandum would not follow from the explanans and the truth of the explanans would not guarantee the truth of the explanandum. This account was therefore referred to as the *deductive-nomological* (or D-N) model of explanation. When Hempel later articulated the structure of explanations that appeal to natural laws of statistical form, he referred to their conditions as the *inductive-statistical* (or I-S) model of explanation, where explanations of this kind assume the form of inductive rather than of deductive arguments.

Suppose, for example, that we want to explain why Jan's bracelet melted when it was heated to 1063° C. We could do so by observing that Jan's bracelet is gold and that things that are gold melt when they are heated to 1063° or more. By means of extensional logic, this could be formalized as:

(D-N) $(x)(t)[Gxt \rightarrow (Hxt \geq 1063° \text{ C} \rightarrow Mxt^*)]$ General Law
      Gbt' & $Hbt' \geq 1063° \text{ C}$ Initial Conditions
_____
      Mbt'^* Explanandum

where t^* is equal to or later than t (for reasons I will explain later). Thus, this explanation "explains" why Jan's bracelet b melted at t'^* by deducing a description of that phenomenon from a general law asserting that everything that is gold G is such that, if it is heated H to 1063° C or more, then it will melt M, and that Jan's bracelet was made of gold and heated to such a temperature, which satisfies the adequacy conditions for D-N explanations.

General laws of this form, of course, assert that every case of a certain kind (heated gold object) will have a certain outcome (melted gold object). Laws of statistical (or "probabilistic") form, by contrast, assert not that all cases will have the same outcome but rather that different outcomes within a fixed set of possible outcomes will occur with a certain probability. In cases of this kind, a statistical generalization of the form, '$P(A/R)=r$', may serve as the lawlike premise of an inductive argument, where an outcome of the kind displayed by the explanandum could be expected to occur with a degree of nomic expectability [r], which is equal to the probability r.

Suppose, for example, that Sally Brown acquired a streptococcus infection but recovered after the administration of penicillin. Such an outcome might be explained by subsumption by means of a statistical generalization maintaining that the probability of recovery from a streptococcus infection when given penicillin equals .9, where this might be formalized as follows:

(I-S) $P(Rxt^*/Sxt$ & $Pxt) = .9$
      Sst' & Pst' Explanans
      _____ [.9]
      Rst'^* Explanandum

Thus, this explanation "explains" why Sally s recovered at t'^* from her infection by observing Sally had streptococcus S and was given penicillin P, where those with streptococcus who are given penicillin recover R with a probability of .9, which means that her recovery under these conditions was to be expected with a degree of nomic expectability [. . .] equal to .9.

Unfortunately, as Hempel's own investigations disclosed, Sally's nonrecovery might also be "explained" with high probability by taking other conditions into account. Suppose, for example, that Sally just happened to have been infected by a penicillin-resistant strain of streptococcus, where the probability of *non*recovery under these conditions equals .66. Then another explanation formally similar to (I-S) could be advanced that had premises that were logically compatible with those of the first as follows:

(I-S') $\quad P(\text{not-}Rxt^*/Sxt \ \& \ Pxt \ \& \ Nxt) = .66$

Explanans

$$\frac{Sst' \ \& \ Pst' \ \& \ Nst'}{\text{not-}Rst'^*} \quad [.66]$$

Explanandum

Thus, this explanation "explains" why Sally s did *not* recover at t'^* from her infection by noting that Sally had streptococcus S and was given penicillin P, but had a strain that was nonsusceptible to penicillin N, where persons with strains of streptococcus that are nonsusceptible to penicillin who are given penicillin do not recover with a probability of .66, which means that nonrecovery was to be expected with a degree of nomic expectability equal to .66.

Hempel referred to this problem as *the statistical ambiguity of inductive-statistical explanations*. Initially he appealed to Carnap's requirement of total evidence in order to resolve it, but later he abandoned that approach on the ground that "*the point of an explanation is not to provide evidence for the occurrence of the explanandum phenomenon but to exhibit it as nomically expectable*" (Hempel 1968, p. 121; original emphasis). He introduced (several versions of) an epistemic *requirement of maximal specificity*, (or "RMS"), which made I-S but not D-N explanations at most "adequate" *in relation to a knowledge context K*. This distinction implied a profound difference between D-N explanations, which can qualify as true explanations, and I-S explanations, which cannot qualify as true, on Hempel's explication.

This discovery created acute distress for Hempel's covering-law theory, which was built on the assumption that explanations explain their explanandum phenomena by exhibiting them as "nomically expectable." While no specific degree of nomic expectability was required on Hempel's theory for an I-S explanation to be "adequate," Hempel consistently implied that that degree of nomic expectability should be "high." The construction of two logically compatible explanans, both of which conferred high degrees of nomic expectability upon incompatible explananda, therefore came as a severe blow, from which the covering-law theory never fully recovered.

THE STATISTICAL-RELEVANCE MODEL

An alternative conception incorporating frequency criteria of explanatory relevance has been advanced, which promises to solve the problem of statistical ambiguity. The theoretical foundation for this model is the conception of objective probabilities as long-run frequencies.

In retrospect, the problem of the statistical ambiguity of inductive-statistical explanations required an ontic rather than an epistemic resolution. In lieu of a requirement of maximal specificity in relation to a knowledge situation, *K,* Hempel needed an objective conception of reference class homogeneity, for which every member of the reference class has the same probability as every other for each possible outcome. Although Hempel despaired of developing an adequate formal explication for this condition, an alternative approach to explanation was being elaborated by Wesley C. Salmon, whose theory of statistical relevance and statistical explanation would become the apparent successor to the covering-law theory during the 1970s.

Salmon's approach (Salmon 1970) shares Hempel's underlying

commitment to the *frequency interpretation* of probability hypotheses, according to which the probability with which an event of kind *A* occurs within a reference class *R* equals the limiting frequency with which attribute *A* occurs within an infinite sequence of kind *R*. But he does not share Hempel's pessimism over the prospect of developing a completely objective conception of reference class homogeneity. Such a conception would require that any subsequence *S* of the original sequence *R* that is "appropriately selected" yield limiting frequencies for *A* that equal those of the original sequence.

The principal motivation for introducing the *statistical relevance* (S-R) model of explanation is Salmon's conviction that Hempel's theory is founded upon a mistaken conception of explanatory relevance. For Hempel, a property *F* is explanatorily relevant to the occurrence of an attribute *A* if there is a lawful relationship that relates *F* to *A*. If table salt dissolves in water, then so does Morton's table salt, Morton's finest table salt, etc., any of which can thus occur in explanations. This violates what Salmon takes to be a fundamental requirement of adequate explanations, which is that statistically irrelevant properties cannot qualify as explanatorily relevant.

The difficulties confronting Hempel's approach were vividly illustrated by the cold recovery and the birth-control pill examples. Salmon noticed that Bill Black's recovery from his cold within a week after taking vitamin C supplied an adequate explanation on Hempel's criteria, since almost all colds clear up within a week after taking vitamin C. But in fact almost all colds clear up within a week *without* taking vitamin C. And that Black did not become pregnant during the past year could similarly be explained by observing that Black had been taking his wife's birth-control pills all year and that any *man* who takes birth-control pills avoids becoming pregnant.

In order to establish which properties should qualify as explanatorily relevant, Salmon introduced the *statistical-relevance criterion* of explanatory relevance, according to which a property *F* is explanatorily relevant to the occurrence of an attribute *A* within a reference class *R* just in case,

(SRC-1) $P(A/R\&F) = m$ and $P(A/R\& \text{ not-}F) = n$, where $m \neq n$;

that is, just in case the limiting frequency for A in R-and-F differs from the limiting frequency for A in R-and-not-F. Any property F for which corresponding probabilities interpreted as limiting frequencies vary is therefore supposed to be explanatorily relevant to the occurrence of A, relative to R.

This criterion enables Salmon's S-R model to cope with the vitamin C and the birth-control pill cases, for example, a problem that Hempel's I-S model cannot solve. Salmon also rejects the requirement of a high probability relation between the explanans and the explanandum of a statistical explanation on the grounds (i) that it renders the explanation of events that only occur with low probability logically impossible, in principle, and (ii) that Carnap's conception of logical probability, which Hempel initially wanted to employ to account for the meaning of nomic expectability [. . .], is hopelessly unsuited for its intended role within the I-S model. Indeed, Hempel himself would eventually accept both of these objections as valid.

Having rejected Hempel's condition of high probability between explanans and explanandum, however, Salmon went further and even abandoned the covering-law conception of explanations as arguments. Adequate scientific explanations now consist of the partition of the reference class R into various subclasses $R\&F1$ to $R\&Fn$, where each subclass is objectively homogeneous, and the singular event to be explained, such as the occurrence of Axt^* (attribute A of object x at time t^*), is explained by assigning it to the appropriate completely objective homogeneous reference class that includes exactly those statistically relevant properties that were present in this case.

Although Salmon's approach appeared to be promising, it encountered several major problems, which were not unrelated. The first was that, in spite of Salmon's optimism, the requirement of objectively homogeneous reference classes required by Salmon's model has proven exceedingly difficult to define formally. Although Salmon has persisted in the belief that an adequate formal explication is possible, his own efforts to produce one (Salmon 1977 and 1984) have been as unavailing as previous efforts by, for example, Hans Reichenbach, Richard von Mises, and Hempel himself.

The second problem, however, was far more serious. It turns out that statistically relevant properties are not *therefore* explanatorily relevant. Salmon employed a screening-off principle to isolate and eliminate statistically irrelevant properties from the explanans of adequate explanations, where *a property F screens off a property G with respect to A in R* when:

$$(SRC-2)\ P(A/R\ \&\ F\ \&\ G) = P(A/R\ \&\ F\ \&\ \text{not-}G) \neq P(A/R\ \&\ \text{not-}F\ \&\ G).$$

While a falling barometer G can indicate approaching rain A on a summer day R, for example, it is screened off by thunderstorms F as explanatorily irrelevant to that effect, because $P(A/R\ \&\ F\ \&\ G) = P(A/R\ \&\ F\ \&\ \text{not-}G)$, yet thunderstorms are not screened off in turn by a falling barometer, because $P(A/R\ \&\ F\ \&\ G) \neq P(A/R\ \&\ \text{not-}F\ \&\ G)$, which was the appropriate outcome.

Unfortunately, certain other properties might not be "screened off" and turn out to qualify as explanatorily relevant even when they presumably were not. If women whose middle initials began with vowels experienced miscarriages with a different frequency than women whose middle initials began with consonants even after other properties were taken into account, then that property would qualify as statistically relevant and *therefore* as explanatorily relevant in relation to that outcome in that reference class. It became increasingly apparent that Salmon's conditions were not successful as general criteria of explanatory relevance, as he would concede in a new work emphasizing considerations of causation (Salmon 1984, pp. 191–192).

The third was that this superabundance of statistically relevant properties created an inescapable tension between two intuitively compatible but theoretically incompatible desiderata, namely: the statistical relevance criterion of statistical relevance and the conception of statistical explanations as irreducibly statistical. Since every event that occurs during the world's history has a unique description, $F1\ \&\ F2\ \&\ \ldots$, as Hempel had observed, there is no end to possible combinations of properties that might turn out to be statistically relevant to an attribute. But this dictates that the only reference classes that could turn out to be objectively homogeneous were ones for which the probability for an attribute A must be $= 0$ or else $= 1$.

Indeed, in relation to any reference class description relative to which such an attribute occurs with any probability $\neq 0$ or $\neq 1$, there will always be other statistically relevant properties that "make a difference" with respect to the occurrence of any attribute A on statistical relevance criteria. The only explanations that could qualify as adequate relative to statistical relevance criteria were those with degenerate probabilities $= 0$ or $= 1$. But this meant that Salmon's criteria of statistical relevance could not support his conception of statistical explanation. His ontic solution to the problem of statistical ambiguity could not be sustained. The rationale for Hempel's thesis of the epistemic relativity of I-S explanations appeared to be intact.

LONG RUNS AND SINGLE CASES

One of the principal difficulties confronting theories of explanation is to establish the right connection between probabilistic laws and their mani- festations. Probabilities may be viewed as probabilistic dispositions of chance setups rather than as limiting frequencies.

The source of these difficulties was not difficult to discern. Re- liance on criteria of statistical relevance left no room to distinguish correlations from causation. Both Hempel and Salmon were devoted to Hume's conception of the nature of laws, even though they en- dorsed Goodman's findings as indispensable to identify those exten- sional generalizations that should be treated as though they were laws. As we have already discovered, it is different for something to be treated as if it were a law and for it to really be one. A more adequate approach to scientific explanation would depend upon a more adequate conception of the nature of probabilistic laws than the extensional conceptions that were fundamental to Hempel and Salmon.

As it happened, Popper had advanced the conception of proba- bilities as *dispositional properties* during the 1950s. While Hempel was tempted by this approach and suggested the possibility that the meaning of probabilistic dispositions might be captured by introducing probabilistic counterparts of nonprobabilistic reduction sentences (Hempel 1965, pp. 460–461), this was not an approach that he would subsequently pursue, quite likely because of the limitations imposed by his methodological commitment to extensional techniques. Ultimately, the development of an adequate conception of probabilistic laws would depend on the adoption of the kind of intensional methodology that Carnap had anticipated would be required.

The basic idea behind Popper's conception was to view probabilities not as long-run frequencies but rather as tendencies that produce long-run frequencies. The differences are substantial. *Long-run frequencies*, for example, are properties of sequences of events, where long-run probabilities can exist only if the long-run sequences of which they are properties also exist. *Tendencies to produce long-run frequencies,* by comparison, are properties of fixed sets of conditions known as "chance setups" (or as "experimental arrangements") as dispositions that would produce ("bring about" or "cause") their various outcomes to occur with specific limiting frequencies were they subjected to endless repetitions or trials.

Advocates of extensional approaches toward the problem of lawlikeness for probabilistic laws tended to adopt the conception of those laws as counterfactual idealizations. Sequences that did not satisfy the conditions required for a statistical generalization to be a probabilistic law—the existence of a limiting frequency within an infinite sequence—simply did not qualify as "probabilistic laws." Few if any of those sequences that occur during the world's history are infinite rather than finite, and many of those of interest concern situations that might have no actual instances at all. The practice was simply to presume that hypothetical sequences could be constructed without requiring any ontic justification.

Thus, the genius of Popper's approach was that probabilities might be understood as dispositions on a par with other dispositions, where the difference was that these dispositions had relative frequencies rather than constant conjunctions as displays. When probabilities are interpreted as *propensities* rather than as *frequencies*, in other words, then propensity predicates could be viewed as supporting subjunctive and counterfactual conditionals on the basis of dispositional properties just as other dispositional predicates were viewed as supporting subjunctive and counterfactual conditionals. These dispositions would provide an ontic justification for corresponding probabilistic subjunctives and counterfactuals in turn.

While Popper viewed these properties as *long-run* propensities, a variation on this theme invited viewing these properties as *single-case* propensities instead, according to which probabilities are dispositional properties of experimental arrangements (or chance setups) to produce one or another among various outcomes on each singular trial (Fetzer 1971 and 1981). This required a conceptual shift by viewing the value of a probability as the strength of a disposition to produce a specific outcome on a singular trial rather than as a disposition to produce such outcomes with a certain limiting frequency. The single-case conception probabilistically implies that repeated trails of chance setups with the same propensities would produce similar long-run frequencies, but it does not guarantee it.

From such a point of view, probabilistic laws as well as universal laws are essentially of universal form. For a probabilistic law under the propensity interpretation no longer simply affirms that a certain percentage of a reference class also belongs to the attribute class. What it asserts is that every member of the reference class possesses a certain (logically contingent) disposition among its permanent properties. In the case of probabilistic laws, that disposition is of probabilistic strength, while in the case of universal laws, it is of universal strength instead. Thus, their difference is not a matter of how many members possess the property in question but a matter of the strength of the property that is possessed by every member.

The consequences of this conceptual exchange can be illustrated in relation to the problem of defining dispositional predicates. Let us assume that "*IQxt = high*" means that x has a high IQ at t, "*TTxt*" that x takes an IQ test at t, and "*TSxt = 130 to 200*" that x's test score falls between 130 and 200 at t, as before. By employing the subjunctive conditional in place of the material and by acknowledging that many other factors $F1, F2, \ldots, Fn$ may influence our score but do not change our intelligence, we previously arrived at a promising definition of the meaning of "intelligence."

According to that conception, Johnny Jones would have a high IQ if he were to take an IQ test under suitable conditions (having the proper attitude, with no physical impairments, and so on) and he were to score between 130 and 200 on that test, which has been formalized as follows:

(D8) $IQxt = high =$df $(TTxt \& Flxt \& \ldots \& Fnxt) \Rightarrow TSxt = 130 \text{ to } 200$.

There now appear to be at least two ways in which that definition could possibly be improved. One is by acknowledging that this property might turn out to be a disposition of probabilistic strength rather than of universal strength. The other is to make explicit that dispositions can be better formalized by employing causal conditionals and intervals of time instead.

These observations are not unrelated. Intelligence would be a disposition of probabilistic rather than of universal strength if there were test conditions under which corresponding outcomes would occur as probable rather than invariable manifestations of that property. If Johnny might sometimes obtain one score rather than another on the same test under the same relevant conditions, then there might be reason to view this as a probabilistic rather than as a universal disposition. If, once in a while, Johnny might even obtain a score out of the 130 to 200 range, although he had a high IQ, then it would be theoretically important to admit that this property represents a probabilistic rather than universal tendency.

Clearly, Johnny's IQ does not cause him to obtain a certain score, all by itself. When Johnny sits down to take an IQ test, he has to exercise his intelligence over a suitable period of time, using appropriate equipment (pencils, paper, and so on), marking his answers and submitting his exam when time has lapsed (rather than tearing it up, turning it into a paper airplane, and so forth). Thus, the property under consideration—like every other disposition—should be envisioned as a property by virtue of which, under suitable conditions, one or another of various effects would be produced by those conditions over an interval of time. A more adequate formalization should reflect this temporal difference.

Both of these considerations invite the introduction of causal conditionals of universal and of probabilistic strength, where '$\ldots =u\!\gg$ ___' stands for a causal tendency of universal strength u and '$\ldots =p\!\gg$ ___' indicates a causal tendency of probabilistic strength p. The role of p, however, is quite different from that of u, since 'p' is a variable which can assume any value between 0 and 1 inclusively as specific instances. When "$IQxt = high$" is envisioned as a universal strength disposition, for example, then the definiens of (D8) ought to be replaced by the following:

(D9) $IQxt = high =$df $(TTxt \, \& \, Flxt \, \& \ldots \& \, Fnxt) =u\!\gg TSxt^*$
        $= 130 \text{ to } 200,$

where time t^* is simultaneous with or subsequent to time t by some fixed interval. But if it is envisioned as a probabilistic disposition instead, then:

(D10) $IQxt = high =$df $(TTxt \, \& \, Flxt \, \& \ldots \& \, Fnxt) =p\!\gg$
        $TSxt^* = 130 \text{ to } 200$

where the variable 'p' is replaced by some suitable value between 0 and 1.

THE CAUSAL-RELEVANCE MODEL

An alternative model that incorporates causal criteria of explanatory relevance has been advanced, which yields the appropriate relations of laws to singular events. The theoretical foundation for this model is the conception of objective probabilities as single-case propensities.

As Salmon had recognized, the problem of the statistical ambiguity of statistical explanations requires an ontic rather than an epistemic resolution. The problem was that Salmon's approach on the basis of statistical relevance criteria provided an ontic solution that was incompatible with the existence of irreducibly statistical explanations. The single-case propensity approach now promised a more adequate conception, where Salmon's requirement of objective homogeneity would be displaced by an ontic version of Hempel's requirement of maximal specificity within the context of a single-case propensity theory of explanation (Fetzer 1974).

The single-case propensity account supports a *causal relevance* (C-R) model of explanation, which is based upon the *causal relevance criterion* of explanatory relevance, according to which a property F is causally relevant to the occurrence of A in relation to reference property R just in case:

(CRC-1) $(Rxt\&Fxt) = m \gg Axt^*$ and $(Rxt\& \text{not-}Fxt) = n \gg Axt^*$, where $m \neq n$;

that is, just in case the strength of the tendency for conditions Rxt-and-Fxt to bring about attribute A on a single trial differs from the strength of the tendency for conditions Rxt-and-not-Fxt to bring about that same attribute, where the relations between these properties must be logically contingent.

This means that frequencies display but do not define probabilities as propensities and that statistical-relevance relations can serve as evidence in relation to causal-relevance hypotheses. Under this conception, lawlike sentences are true only when they are "maximally specific" by specifying within their antecedents the presence or absence of every property that makes a difference to the occurrence of attribute A. Unlike Hempel's conception, however, this *requirement of maximal specificity* is a completely objective condition whose satisfaction is independent of a knowledge context K. The analysis appeals to a different notion of logical probability in place of Carnap's and preserves the view of explanations as arguments.

The conditions of adequacy that attend this account are strikingly similar to those of Hempel's original conditions for D-N explanation, with several exceptions accommodating probabilistic counterparts within the context of an ontic explication. Thus, in comparison with Hempel's I-S model and Salmon's S-R model, the most important feature of the C-R model is its appeal to an intensional rather than an extensional conception of natural laws. The development of a formal calculus of the kind that Carnap envisioned, no doubt, is a difficult and challenging enterprise, but it can be pursued as a branch of formal semantics (Fetzer 1981, Ch. 3, and Fetzer 1988).

Moreover, in order to handle the problem of irrelevant properties, an adequate explication also requires the adoption of a condition to exclude causally (or, more generally, "nomically") irrelevant properties from the explanans of an adequate explanation. Salmon's screening-off condition is replaced by another restricting the predicates appearing in an explanans:

(CRC-2)   A predicate 'Fi' can appear in the antecedent of a lawlike premise S of an explanans only if it is causally (or nomically) relevant to the phenomenon that is described by the explanandum-sentence.

This should be referred to as the *requirement of strict maximal specificity.*

An additional advantage of the single-case propensity approach is that it yields an elegant solution to the underlying problem of objective homogeneity, where the statistical-relevance conception is replaced by a causal-relevance counterpart, according to which a sequence of trials is *physically random* if and only if the causally (or nomically) relevant properties that affect each of its trial members do not vary from trial to trial (Fetzer 1981, pp. 111–114). This reflects yet one more benefit of a conception of probability that takes single cases as fundamental and generates short and long runs of relative and limiting frequencies as repeated trials of those kinds.

The requirement of maximal specificity (RMS) itself insures that every sentence that describes a law can be true only when the presence or absence of every property whose presence or absence makes a difference to the occurrence of the outcome of interest is included in the antecedent of that law, which is satisfied when they are explicitly mentioned or logically implied. The requirement of strict maximal specificity (RSMS) further insures that only properties whose presence or absence makes a difference to the occurrence of the outcome of interest can be included in the antecedent of laws that appear in the premises of arguments that are intended to be explanatory. Explanatory adequacy requires that both conditions be fulfilled.

Indeed, once this additional condition has been acknowledged, it is possible to formalize the requirements that an adequate explanation must satisfy. Explanations are still arguments that have premises and conclusions, where adequate explanations must satisfy the following general conditions:

(CA-1′) the explanandum must be a deductive or a probabilistic consequence of its explanans;

(CA-2′) the explanans must contain at least one lawlike sentence that is actually required for the deductive or probabilistic derivation of the explanandum from its explanans;

(CA-3′) the explanation must satisfy the requirement of strict maximal specificity with respect to its lawlike premises; and,

(CA-4′) the sentences constituting the explanation—both the explanans and the explanandum—must be true.

Thus, the combined effect of these requirements insures that the lawlike premises of an adequate explanation must specify all and only those properties whose presence or absence made a difference to the occurrence of its explanandum-phenomenon [Fetzer (1981), pp. 126–127; cf. Fetzer (1983)].

While Salmon viewed deductive explanations as a special limiting case of statistical explanations that would occur when the limiting frequency of attribute A in reference class $R = m/n = 1$ (when $m = n$), Hempel differentiated between D-N and I-S explanations as distinctive in kind, not only because one was ontic and the other epistemic, but also because D-N explanations were formalizable as deductive arguments, while I-S explanations were not. The causal-relevance model maintains the view that there are two kinds of C-R explanation, which differ in the kind of law appearing in them and in the kind of argument that is required for their formalization.

Suppose, once again, that we want to explain why Jan's bracelet melted when it was heated to 1063° C. We could do so by observing that Jan's bracelet is gold and that things that are gold melt when they are heated to 1063° C or more. By means of intensional logic, this could be formalized as a *universal-deductive* explanation that would exemplify the following form:

$$(\text{U-D}) \quad (x)(t)[Gxt \Rrightarrow (Hxt \geq 1063° \text{ C} = u \Rrightarrow Mxt^*)]$$

$$\underline{Gbt' \ \& \ Hbt' \geq 1063° \text{ C}}$$

$$Mbt'^* \qquad\qquad [u]$$

with labels: the first two lines as Explanans, the last as Explanandum.

where the single line between explanans and explanandum indicates that the explanandum cannot be false if its explanans is true, and the symbol in brackets indicates that this explanandum occurs in relation to this explanans with a degree of nomic expectability that is of universal strength.

Or suppose, once again, that Sally Brown incurred a streptococcus infection but recovered after the administration of penicillin. Such an outcome could be explained by subsumption by means of a probabilistic law that maintains that the probability of recovery from a streptococcus infection when given penicillin equals .9, where this might be formalized as, say, a *universal-probabilistic* explanation that exemplifies the following form:

$$(\text{U-P}) \quad (x)(t)[Sxt \Rrightarrow (Pxt = .9 \Rrightarrow Rxt^*)]$$

$$\underline{Sst' \ \& \ Pst'}$$

$$Rst'^* \qquad\qquad [.9]$$

with labels: the first two lines as Explanans, the last as Explanandum.

where the double line between explanans and explanandum means that the explanandum can still be false even if the explanans is true, and the symbol in brackets indicates this explanandum occurs relative to this explanans with a degree of nomic expectability of probabilistic strength .9.

Perhaps it ought to be emphasized that (RMS) and (RSMS) combine to preclude the possibility of explanatory ambiguities of any kind for deductive or probabilistic arguments, which must take into account all and only explanatorily relevant properties to qualify as adequate. If Sally had been infected by a penicillin-resistant strain of streptococcus (or had contracted AIDS, and so on), that would have to be included in an adequate explanans. The corresponding law thus determines the degree of nomic expectability with which the truth of the conclusion should be expected given the truth of the premises. It thereby forges the link between explanations and expectations.

Since a probabilistic law assigning a propensity of strength p to an outcome of kind A must have a counterpart assigning a propensity of strength equal to or less than $1-p$ to an outcome of kind not-A, relative to the same conditions R, the occurrence of a phenomenon or its nonoccurrence can be explained by citing precisely the same relevant conditions! (Cf. Salmon 1984, pp. 277–278.) This seems surprising until you consider that, in cases of this kind, all and only those properties whose presence or absence was nomically responsible for bringing those outcomes about have been cited. Nothing more and nothing less can be asked of an adequate scientific explanation.

QUESTIONS ABOUT EXPLANATIONS

Several important questions remain to be addressed, including whether explanations have to be explicit in order to be adequate. There is more to an explanation than an inference from law, for example, and not all explanations are causal. A number of these issues are considered here.

The relations between explanations and predictions are going to be considered further in Chapter Five. Before turning to matters of probability and inference, it may be worthwhile to explore the ramifications of the causal-relevance model for several fundamental questions about the nature of explanation in science. Some of these questions concern matters that we are going to explore in detail in chapters to follow. In this section, I shall raise some of the more important issues that the previous discussion has not yet addressed in the expectation of shedding more light on this central subject.

Q1: Are explanations nothing but inferences from laws?

No. Although Hempel assumed, for example, that valid deductions from general laws were always explanatory, that assumption was mistaken. The flagpole example, which we shall consider, was among the first indications that Hempel was wrong, but other cases are, in certain respects, even more compelling. The generalization that anyone run over by a steamroller dies no doubt qualifies as a natural law. From that lawlike premise and the observation that you are alive, we can infer that you have not been run over by a steamroller. But that would hardly explain why. Hempel focused his attention upon arguments involving *modus ponens*, but others involving *modus tollens* are no less valid and in many ways much more instructive.

Q2: Are explanations always causal in their character?

No. Salmon has frequently asserted that explanations are not adequate unless they are causal. His motto has been, "Let's put the 'cause' back into 'because'!" (Salmon 1979). But there are ample illustrations that Salmon's cause is not going to be victorious. Consider, for example, any relationship between two properties, such as that (pure) gold is malleable. We can perfectly properly explain why something is malleable by subsuming it as an instance of (pure) gold by means of that generalization. So long as generalizations of this kind qualify as lawlike—and when they involve permanent properties, they appear to be perfect examples—these cases illustrate simple ("nomic") forms of possible explanations satisfying (CA-1′) to (CA-4′).

The lawlike sentences that appear in explanations of this simple kind are always merely subjunctive and never causal in conditionality, where these properties are properties that are nomically rather than causally related. Such explanations display the classic structure of D-N explanations:

$$(\text{D-N}') \qquad (x)(t)(Gxt \gg Mxt) \qquad \qquad \text{Explanans}$$
$$Gbt'$$
$$\overline{\qquad\qquad\qquad\qquad}$$
$$Mbt' \qquad\qquad\qquad\qquad \text{Explanandum}$$

Informally expressed, this asserts that (pure) gold is malleable and that Jan's bracelet is gold, which explains why it is malleable. The omission of the bracketed symbol further indicates that it is not a causal explanation.

Q3: Are explanations always formal in formulation?

No. Although it is not difficult to imagine that you may have drawn an inference of this kind on the basis of my discussions, *explanations as they are advanced in technical scientific and in ordinary conversational contexts are typically expressed in partial and elliptical form.* The point of a model of explanation is to make explicit conditions of adequacy whose satisfaction guarantees that an explanation qualifies as "adequate." The role of contextual factors in conversations includes presuppositions concerning shared beliefs about explanation situations that make it unnecessary to always be so explicit. Informal conversational explanations may be perfectly acceptable, provided that those explanations implicitly satisfy the relevant conditions.

Q4: Are some explanations "theoretical explanations?"

Yes. The distinctive feature of a theoretical explanation appears to be that its explanandum is a generalization rather than a singular event. Explanations of both kinds seem to satisfy the same conditions of adequacy. An example of a theoretical explanation exhibiting the distinctive features of the intension conception that I am elaborating would be the following:

1. $(x)(t)(Gxt \gg Mxt)$ General Law
2. $\Box(x)(t)[Mxt \rightarrow (HSxt =u\gg RSxt^*)]$ Definition
3. $(x)(t)[Gxt \gg (HSxt =u\gg RSxt^*)]$ General Law

Figure 5. A Scientific Theory

Informally expressed, this asserts that, if gold things G are malleable M and if malleable things are things for which hammering them into a shape HS brings about their retaining that shape RS at that time, then anything that is gold would be such that hammering it into a certain shape would bring about its retaining that shape at that time (cf. Fetzer 1981, Ch. 6).

Theories are envisioned as sets of laws and definitions that apply to a common domain. Indeed, the abstract structure of Figure 5 is as follows:

1. $(x)(t)(Wxt \gg Xxt)$ Axiom
2. $\Box(x)(t)[Xxt \rightarrow (Yxt =u\gg Zxt)]$ Axiom
3. $(x)(t)[Wxt \gg (Yxt =u\gg Zxt)]$ Theorem

Figure 6. Its Abstract Structure

Comparison with similar figures in Chapter Three suggests that the intensional conception provides a partial vindication of the standard conception. This is not a difficult hypothesis to evaluate, because the primary differences that distinguish them have to do with the logical features of the abstract calculi that they endorse rather than with their empirical interpretations.

Q5. And what about the problem of provisoes?

The condition that lawlike sentences must have antecedents that are maximally specific to be true appears to afford a promising solution to the problem of provisoes. The laws formulated by idealized theories can be employed to explain the behavior of actual things only when those things happen to satisfy the conditions they specify. Even idealized laws as counterfactual generalizations whose antecedents have no instances can be supplemented by less-idealized laws as subjunctive generalizations whose antecedents might have instances. The existence of such simple idealized laws does not preclude the discovery of more complex laws as science advances.

Q6. Is there a new consensus about explanation?

The answer is not entirely clear. During the 1980s, the single-case propensity approach assumed increasing prominence in philosophical discussions of explanation. Salmon halfway abandoned the S-R model in favor of the C-R model, envisioning statistical-relevance relations as "evidence" for causal-relevance relations (Salmon 1984, pp. 22–23). Recent work on explanation suggests that the situation has not settled down sufficiently to maintain that there is a "new consensus" (Kitcher and Salmon 1989). But there are reasons to think that the unified theory of law and explanation it supports will steadily continue to gain ground (Fetzer 1991b and 1992).

An adequate theory of scientific explanation could not be provided in the absence of an adequate theory of probabilistic laws. The long-run frequency conception was unable to cope with the single case. A more successful model appeals to the single-case propensity account instead.

CHAPTER FIVE

PROBABILITY AND INFERENCE

A mong the most important problems in the development of an adequate model of science is understanding the inferential relations among three different kinds of probabilities, which affords a foundation for understanding how probability can serve as "a guide in life."

THE SYMMETRY THESIS

According to the symmetry thesis, every adequate explanation could have served as a basis for prediction and every adequate prediction could have served as a basis for explanation. Many reasons suggest that this specific hypothesis, although plausible, cannot be sustained.

As we have now discovered, the approach that supplies the C-R model of causal explanation applies to simple ("nomic") explanations and to theoretical explanations as well as to universal-deductive and universal-probabilistic explanations. The single-case propensity approach can cope with the problem of objective homogeneity (by means of the definition of physical randomness). Its application can generate reference classes with nontrivial probabilities between 0 and 1 (because it is not restricted to statistical relevance criteria). And the conditions of adequacy that are imposed by C-R explanations do not stand in conflict with C-R criteria of relevance.

The extent to which conditions of this kind "make a difference" to the theory of explanation can be illustrated in relation to *the symmetry thesis.* In his classic paper with Oppenheim, Hempel asserted that the structure of explanations and predictions was the same, where the only difference between them is pragmatic: explanations explain why a past event occurred, while predictions anticipate an event in the future. Thus, "an explanation of a particular event is not fully adequate unless its explanans, if taken account of in time, could have served as a basis for predicting the event in question," and conversely (Hempel and Oppenheim 1948, pp. 138–139).

Strictly speaking, therefore, the symmetry thesis is equivalent to the conjunction of two distinct subtheses, which can be expressed as follows:

(ST-1)   *every adequate explanation is potentially an adequate prediction.*

(ST-2)   *every adequate prediction is potentially an adequate explanation.*

The conditions that explanations and predictions were supposed to fulfill, however, were supposed to be the very same, namely, (CA-1) to (CA-4). Consequently, it would be possible to embrace a "qualified version" of the symmetry thesis by accepting (ST-1) while rejecting (ST-2), for example, which eventually became Hempel's position (Hempel 1965, pp. 367–376).

Indeed, during the 1960s, Sylvain Bromberger's flagpole example and Michael Scriven's paresis example already hinted that it could not be sustained. The paresis example counts against the symmetry thesis because only about 25% of those who contract syphilis develop paresis, yet 100% of those who develop paresis do so because they have syphilis. Thus, this case seems to support an explanation for paresis, yet it does not support the corresponding prediction that paresis will occur. It therefore suggests that some adequate explanations may not be potential predictions, which does nothing to enhance the plausibility of subthesis (ST-1).

The flagpole example was telling against the symmetry thesis because the length of a shadow cast by a flagpole together with the laws of the rectilinear propagation of light and some principles of geometry support the inference that the flagpole that casts such a shadow must have a specific height h, yet surely does not explain why it possesses that height. (Presumably, it has that height because it was constructed a certain length l and implanted into the ground to a depth d, thereby extending above the ground to a height h [$= l - d$]. This case thus violated the subthesis (ST-2).

Bromberger's example had more immediate impact, no doubt because it so clearly contravened the covering-law conception of explanations as arguments from premises including laws. The Scriven case was greeted with less enthusiasm, probably because the precise requirements that an adequate I-S explanation had to satisfy were not as well understood. The flagpole case thus stood as a clear exception to Hempel's D-N model, while the paresis case stood as a not entirely clear possible exception to Hempel's I-S model. In retrospect, however, the paresis case appears to be at least as revealing as the flagpole case for several different reasons.

In the first place, the paresis case implies that events that occur only with low probability are incapable of being explained by any model that requires events to have a probability that is "high" in order to be explained. Thus, Salmon has recently suggested that Scriven deserves the honor of having implicitly established the untenability of Hempel's requirement of a "high" logical probability relating an I-S explanans to its explanandum. In the second place, however, it also hints that "nomic expectability" might not be the same thing as "nomic predictability," an ancient ambiguity with substantial consequences for understanding Hempel's theory of explanation.

The fundamental desideratum of Hempel's theory of explanation is that explanations explain by displaying the *nomic expectability* of their explanandum-phenomena. Motivated by the symmetry thesis and by the problem of the statistical ambiguity of I-S explanations, he imposed the "high" probability requirement. But while a probability equal to or greater than .5 might be essential to principles of prediction, those values are not essential to principles of explanation. Thus, abandoning the "high probability" requirement does not mean abandoning the "nomic expectability" desideratum, because "expectability" and "predictability" are separable notions.

Consider, for example, the probabilistic explanation of why Sally

Brown did not recover from a streptococcus infection, even after the administration of penicillin. If recovery occurs under these conditions with a probability of .9, after all, non-recovery must occur under these conditions with a probability of .1, as a matter of mathematics. Such an explanation could be asserted as a *universal-probabilistic* explanation of the following form:

(U-P') $(x)(t)[Sxt \Rightarrow (Pxt = .1 \Rightarrow \text{not-}Rxt^*)]$ Explanans

$Sst' \& Pst'$
$$\overline{\hspace{6cm}} [.1]$$
not-Rst'^* Explanandum

where the symbol in brackets indicates such an explanans confers a degree of nomic expectability upon its explanandum of the probabilistic strength .1.

In general, the occurrence of an outcome of a certain kind is predicted if its probability is greater than .5, because then its probability is "high" and no other outcome of another kind can also have "high" probability. But in cases of the kind displayed by (U-P'), surely we know enough to expect the occurrence of non-recovery with a probability of .1, even though we would predict the occurrence of recovery, because outcomes of that kind have the probability .9. When the expectation for rain is low, we may have a picnic in the expectation that it will not rain, but take our rain coats "just in case." Nomic expectability and nomic predictability are related but distinct ideas.

To understand the connection between them, notice that the adequacy of *predictions* presupposes high nomic expectability, insofar as predicting the occurrence of an event presumes that its probability is "high enough" to warrant the assumption that it will occur. The sense of "prediction" at issue here, of course, is *rational prediction*; bettors at racetracks regularly think of their bets as "predictions," when they are properly understood as wagering on the basis of "expectations." The situation is therefore considerably different with respect to the adequacy of *explanations*, because explaining the occurrence of an event of a certain kind does not assume, for example, that no alternative result has a higher probability of occurrence.

Indeed, high nomic expectability is neither necessary nor sufficient for explanatory adequacy, as we have already implicitly discovered. The flagpole example and the steamroller case both illustrate that inferences from laws, even ones with high nomic expectability, are not always explanatory. Moreover, while high nomic expectability may be sufficient for predictive adequacy, it does not appear to be necessary. If predictive inferences can be based upon correlations rather than causation, for example, then inferences without laws might still be predictive. The principal benefit of the causal-relevance model from this perspective seems to be that it replaces the desideratum of nomic expectability with that of nomic responsibility.

The causal-relevance model fulfills the desideratum of *nomic responsibility* by insuring that an explanation qualifies as "adequate" only provided that it takes into account every property whose presence or absence is responsible for explanandum-phenomena of that kind. The combination of the requirement of maximal specificity with the requirement of strict maximal specificity guarantees that explanations "explain" by specifying all and only those factors whose presence contributed to their outcomes. When the difference between "prediction" and "expectation" is properly understood, therefore, it becomes entirely evident that, even in its qualified form as (ST-1), the symmetry thesis cannot possibly be sustained.

CHANCE AND GAMES OF CHANCE

Games of chance can be understood in terms of elementary axioms of the theory of probability. These include that probabilities have values between 0 and 1, that the values of probabilities for a set of outcomes sum to 1, and that some probabilities are conditional.

Almost everyone in the United States grows up playing various kinds of "games of chance." Some involve coins, others dice, still others cards. Most of us thereby acquire a familiarity with principles of probability, even if we do not know them by that name. Thus, we discover that two-sided coins have a chance for heads and a chance for tails, which may or may not be the same. When they are the same, there is a 50% chance of heads and a 50% chance of tails. If the circumstances under which coins are tossed permit them occasionally to land on their sides, for example, these chances would be somewhat different. If the coin happens to be bent or to be two-headed, then those chances may be greatly different.

In the case of dice, we learn that a normal die has six sides (showing an ace, a deuce, and so on), where fair dice are those for which each possible outcome has an equal chance when they are properly tossed. When this happens, each side has a $1/6$ chance of coming up on a single toss of the die. If the die happens to be loaded by having a small weight inside, for example, then the chances for these outcomes are not the same. Whether the dice are loaded or not, however, the chances of each of the possible outcomes, on any single toss, when added together must sum to 1, just as whether the coin is bent or not, the chances for each possible outcome, on any single toss, when added together must sum to 1. Always!

Since the chances for the different possible outcomes must sum to 1, we can easily calculate the chances of various possible outcomes if only we know their chances. If we know the chance for heads equals $1/3$ because the coin is bent, we know that the chance for tails must be $2/3$. If we know that the chance for a showing a six equals $1/3$ because the die is loaded, we know that the chance for a non-six (for other-than-a-six) must equal $2/3$. If we know that the chances for each outcome equals $1/6$, then we can calculate the chances for an ace or a deuce as equal to the chance of an ace plus the chance of a deuce (or $1/6$ plus $1/6 = 1/3$).

Card games are especially instructive, because the combinations of possible outcomes provide a richer assortment of examples. Consider, for example, that a standard deck has 52 cards divided into four suits (spades, hearts, diamonds, and clubs) of 13 cards apiece, consisting of A, K, Q, J, 10, 9, 8, 7, 6, 5, 4, 3, and 2. When a deck of cards is given a "random" shuffle (which, with a new deck, will take about seven shuffles), then the chance for the Q of clubs, for example, equals the chance for getting the Q when you have a club multiplied by the chance for a club. Since there is only one Q in the club suit and there are 13 clubs out of 52 cards, the chance for the Q of clubs on a single draw is $1/52$.

The same result, however, can also be calculated by observing that the chance for the Q of clubs is equal to the chance for obtaining a club when you have a Q. Since there are 4 Qs out of 52 cards and only 1 of them is a club, the chance of getting the Q of clubs also equals $4/52 \times 1/4 = 1/52$. Notice that there are two different ways of making such a calculation. Putting the matter more abstractly, the chances of getting both an A and a B equal the chance of getting an A when you have a B times the chance of getting a B. But they are also equal to the chance of getting a B when you have an A times the chance of getting an A.

Believe it or not, these simple examples already illustrate the basic principles of probability. The first is that every outcome has a chance that falls somewhere between 0 and 1. (Your chance for tails equals 0 with a two-headed coin!) This makes the values of chance real numbers that fall within the unit interval. The second is that, when you add chances for all of the various possible distinct outcomes together, they must sum to 1. (The chance for getting an ace, a deuce, and so on, must add up to 1, whether or not that die is fair!) When values fulfill this relationship, they can be said to satisfy a principle of summation.

The third is that the chance for obtaining either one outcome or another but not both equals the chance of getting the first *plus* the chance of getting the second. (The chance for a head or a tail with a fair coin that cannot land on its side equals $1/2 + 1/2 = 1$. The chance for an ace or a deuce equals the chance for an ace plus the chance for a deuce, or $1/6 + 1/6 = 1/3$, when that die is fair. The chance for a king or queen equals $4/52 + 4/52 = 2/13$ with a normal deck that has been properly shuffled. And so forth.) The fulfillment of this property, moreover, means that chances can also be said to satisfy a principle of additivity.

The fourth is that the chance for getting an outcome of one kind and of another *together* (when both are possible) equals the chance of getting the second when you already have the first *times* the chance of getting the first. And yet it also equals the chance of getting the first when you already have the second *times* the chance of getting the second. (Thus, to advance a simpler example, the chance of getting an ace and an odd outcome equals the chance of getting an ace when you have an odd outcome times the chance of getting an odd outcome [or $1/3 \times 1/2 = 1/6$]. But it also equals the chance of getting an odd outcome when you have an ace times the chance of getting an ace [or $1/1 \times 1/6 = 1/6$]. Really!)

There are other principles involved here, but for now these will do. The fourth principle we have considered is known as the definition of *conditional probability*. Values that satisfy all four of these conditions are commonly known as "conditional probabilities." Now it is tempting to suppose that "chances" ought to be identified with either long-run frequencies or with single-case propensities. Before addressing questions of this kind, however, ask yourself what kinds of explanations or predictions apply in the case of games of chance. Take card games as the example. When you win a game of gin rummy, could your success have been explained? And, could your success have been predicted?

The answers to these questions, of course, are not difficult to see. The result of a deal with a normal deck is an effect that has been determined by the relative locations of the cards after they have been shuffled. There is no mystery in explaining why you got exactly the cards you were dealt as a function of the arrangement of the cards in the deck and the number of persons in the game. But this means that, in principle, if you had knowledge of those conditions—which the rules of the game do not permit (it is called "cheating")—you could have predicted in each case exactly who would receive each card that was dealt. The only kind of "chance" involved here is a function of our ignorance.

The situation is similar in the case of flips of coins or of tosses of dice, even though it looks very different. If we were in the position to make sufficiently precise measurements of the exact forces imparted to coins and dice on tosses (the exact conditions of those tosses, including the distance to where they would land, and so on), then relying upon the laws of physics, we could probably do a pretty good job of predicting whether they would come up heads or show an ace.

The rules of the game do not allow it, however, and it would take a great effort to carry it out. (We normally have better things to do with our time!)

These cases, too, appear to be ones in which "chances" exist only as a function of our ignorance. The kinds of explanations that would be appropriate in cases of these kinds appear to be universal-deductive rather than universal-probabilistic. But that seems very odd. Surely chances have something to do with probabilities! The question thus becomes whether it might be possible to have a theory about chance. It is easy to show that relative frequencies in finite sequences satisfy all four principles. It is more difficult to show that limiting frequencies in infinite sequences satisfy all four principles. But it is impossible to show that single-case propensities satisfy all four principles.

DETERMINISM AND INDETERMINISM

While traditional games of chance can be properly interpreted by means of the frequency conception, the discovery of indeterministic phenomena in quantum mechanics invites an interpretation of probabilistic causation only the propensity conception can supply.

The problem for propensities is not just that these are theoretical properties that cannot be measured simply but the more striking one that single-case propensities do not qualify as conditional probabilities. The problem is that, as single-case causal tendencies, propensities cannot satisfy the definition of conditional probability. When formally expressed, this condition relates some probabilities to other probabilities:

(CP) $P(A\&B) = P(A/B) \times P(B) = P(B/A) \times P(A)$;

which asserts that the probability for the joint occurrence of A and B is equal to the probability of A, given B, times the probability for B, and is also equal to the probability of B, given A, times the probability of A.

Single-case propensities relate trials on chance setups (or experimental arrangements) to their probabilistic outcomes, where the relation between trials and outcomes is that of probabilistic causes to their effects. While it makes sense for there to be propensities from causes to their probabilistic effects, however, the opposite does not make any sense at all. Substitute effect "E" for "A" and cause "C" for "B" in (CP):

(CP′) $P(E \& C) = P(E/C) \times P(C) = P(C/E) \times P(E).$

If propensities were conditional probabilities, then it would have to be the case that, for every case in which there exists a propensity for certain conditions C to produce an outcome E, $P(E/C)$, there also exists a propensity for that outcome E to produce those same conditions C, $P(C/E)$.

At least two aspects of this surprising situation should be emphasized. The first is that propensities *are* "conditional" in the sense that they are relative to specific conditions. The question here is not whether or not they are relative to specific conditions, which is true, but whether or not they are *symmetrical*, where whenever there is a propensity from A to B there is also a propensity from B to A, which is not true. The second is that the difficulty encountered here by single-case propensities would also be encountered by any other conception of probability as a causal tendency. It arises from having a notion that integrates probability with causation.

An example that reflects the temporal parameters involved here may serve to bring this point home. Remember Sally, who recovered from a streptococcus infection after being treated with penicillin? If we rely on the same formalism as before, this instance of (CP′) would look like this:

(CP″) $P[Rst^* \& (Sst' \& Pst')] = P(Rst^*/Sst' \& Pst') \times P(Sst' \& Pst') = P(Sst' \& Pst'/Rst^*) \times P(Rst^*).$

If propensities were probabilities in the sense of (CP), then it would have to be possible for there to exist propensities for Sally's infection and treatment, given her recovery, as well as propensities for her recovery, given her infection and treatment. But these "inverse propensities" do not exist.

The only cases in which it makes sense to talk about "inverse causes" would seem to be those of laws of coexistence, such as the ideal gas law, for which $PV = nRT$, where the pressure P times the volume V of an ideal gas equals its n moles times its temperature T and a universal constant R. In cases of this kind, it might or might not be reasonable to maintain that the right-hand side "causes" the left-hand side and that the left-hand side also "causes" the right-hand side. Opinions differ (cf. Fetzer 1981, pp. 144–146). But there appears to be no difference of opinion about the situation with respect to whether or not propensities satisfy the definition of conditional probably: they do not! (See Salmon 1984 and Humphreys 1985.)

The appropriate response to adopt when confronted with this problem, however, is another question entirely. Even if propensities cannot satisfy both "direct" and "inverse" probability values, they do satisfy principles of addition, summation, and multiplication. Perhaps this simply means that they are nonstandard probabilities, which does not preclude their importance *even as interpretations of probability*! Non-Euclidean geometry first emerged as a nonstandard conception of geometry, but its significance is none the less for that. Any conception of probability as a causal tendency that qualified as a conditional probability could not be adequate, which is why propensity hypotheses have distinctive syntax (Fetzer 1981, Part I).

This discovery appears to be especially important when our attention shifts from games of chance to quantum mechanics, where a wide range of phenomena display indeterministic behavior. A suitable illustration is the laws of radioactive decay. Just as gold is malleable, polonium[218] has a half-life of 3.05 minutes. Interpreting this property as a frequency, it designates an amount of time during which approximately half the atoms in a reference population would decay. Interpreting this property as a propensity instead, it asserts that the propensity for a single atom of polonium[218] to decay during a temporal interval of 3.05 minutes equals $1/2$.

In order to explain the occurrence of an outcome of this kind, therefore, an explanation could be constructed concerning a specific atom a of polonium[218] that explains why that atom decayed between time t and $t + 3.05$ minutes on the basis of the probabilistic law that every atom of polonium[218] is such that, were it subject to any temporal interval of 3.05 minutes duration, then its propensity to decay during that interval would equal $1/2$. Such an explanation would assume the same form as any other (U-P) explanation: its adequacy depends on satisfying (RMS), where there are no other properties whose presence or absence would make a difference to this propensity (such as nuclear bombardment in the meanwhile).

Now, strictly speaking, the satisfaction of the requirement of maximal specificity means that the system thereby described is a "closed system" in relation to the occurrence of its outcomes. *Closed systems* are ones for which no condition that makes a difference to their behavior has been excluded from their specification. Closed systems where the same outcomes are invariably produced by the same tests under the same conditions are *deterministic*. Closed systems where various outcomes are produced by the same tests under the same conditions are *indeterministic*. So atoms of polonium[218] are indeterministic systems with respect to their decay.

When these distinctions are applied to radioactivity, on the one hand, and to games of chance, on the other, the situation appears to be the following. When games of chance qualify as closed systems, they turn out to be deterministic systems that are only "chance phenomena" as a function of our ignorance. When radioactive atoms qualify as closed systems, they turn out to be indeterministic systems that are "chance phenomena" in a far stronger sense. The conception of probabilities as frequencies appears appropriate for games of chance, while the conception of probabilities as propensities appears appropriate for radioactive atoms. Indeed, the differences that we have uncovered reinforce the distinction (Fetzer 1983).

FREQUENCIES, PROPENSITIES, AND PERSONAL PROBABILITIES

The central problems of scientific inference involve understanding the relations between probabilities as frequencies, as propensities, and as personal probabilities. There are reasons to think that subjective probabilities ought to be based upon objective probabilities.

What we have discovered is that relative frequencies (for heads, deuces, and the like) can be the expectable result of *different deterministic arrangements* (of coin tosses, throws of dice, and so forth). Every time we "cut the cards" we are dealing with a closed system for which, when every relevant property is taken into account, the same conditions always produce the same result. Even when we are ignorant of maximally specific descriptions of conditions in each case or do not know the laws that govern deterministic systems of those kinds, we might still possess knowledge about corresponding frequencies that could be suitable for making frequency-based predictions.

We have also discovered that relative frequencies (for recovery, and the like) can be the expectable result of *similar indeterministic arrangements* (of infections with treatment, and so on). Every time an atom of polonium[218] is subject to a "time trial," we are dealing with a closed system for which, even when every relevant property is taken into account, the same conditions can yield one result (decay) on one occasion and another (no decay) on another. When we possess knowledge of maximally specific descriptions of the conditions in each case and know the laws that govern indeterministic systems of those kinds, then we are in the position to advance propensity-based explanations and also in the position to advance propensity-based predictions.

If games of chance involve deterministic systems with frequencies that are functions of our ignorance, the values of those frequencies can be viewed as "subjective probabilities." *Subjective probabilities* are degrees of belief (or strengths of conviction) of persons z at times t as functions of our attitudes toward the world rather than properties of the world itself. Your degree of belief that your team will win the World Series, for example, can differ from my degree of belief that your team will win that event. Since degrees of belief, even when they are probabilistic, do not have to satisfy the conditions that are characteristic of mathematical probabilities (of summation, addition, and multiplication, for example), we can refer to subjective probabilities that *do* satisfy these relations as *personal probabilities*. There is an extensive literature on personal probabilities, much of which becomes very technical very fast. (Cf. Skyrms 1975 and Kyburg and Smokler 1980.)

From the perspective of the philosophy of science, the most interesting question that can be raised about personal probabilities concern their relations to propensities and frequencies. Because propensities and frequencies are properties of the world rather than merely our attitudes toward the world, they are often referred to as *objective probabilities*. Most philosophers who develop theories of belief and decision on the basis of subjective probabilities assign an important role to the principles of probability and especially to Bayes' theorem. Those who accent or emphasize the role of objective probabilities are known as "objective Bayesians," while those who deny or minimize the role of objective probabilities are known as "subjective Bayesians."

Salmon (1988), for example, provides a general account of the manner in which probability can function as a guide in life from the perspective of an objective Bayesian. Salmon identifies probabilities with *frequencies* on the ground that the causal directedness of propensities inhibits them from qualifying as a proper interpretation of the calculus of probability. He endorses the conception of *propensities* as probabilistic causes, elaborating the thesis that, "We can find out about many propensities by observing frequencies." Indeed, he offers a new version of the straight rule of induction, according to which observed frequencies permit inferences about causal propensities.

One of the fascinating features of his study is his analysis of the views of the subjective Bayesian, David Lewis, especially as they are found in a recent paper (Lewis 1980). Much of Salmon's discussion focuses upon the relationship that ought to obtain between beliefs about probabilities and probabilistic beliefs. According to the *Principal Principle* that Lewis has advanced, for example, our "degree of belief" in the assertion that A must always equal the objective probability (or "chance") of A when it is known. But his approach accents the role of subjective probabilities in determining the values of objective chances, which for him are not unique.

Those who really believe in the existence of objective chance, of course, may find Lewis' emphasis somewhat misdirected. In Salmon's estimation, for example, the inferential relations involved here are better understood the other way around, where objective chances determine subjective probabilities. The "objective" element of

Salmon's position thus suggests that our beliefs about probabilities should be based on relative frequencies as evidence in support of beliefs about objective probabilities and personal probabilities. The analysis that he provides is summed up by his dictum, "Respect the frequencies!", as evidence in drawing inferences about them.

One way to view the situation as Salmon sees it is to envision the Lewis principle as implying the evidential irrelevance of any belief E other than those about objective chance X in determining one's degree of belief in A. So it qualifies as a *subjective-probability criterion* of rational irrelevance:

(SPC) $C(A/X\&E) = x = C(A/X\& \text{not-}E)$;

that is, one's subjective probability (or "credence") C in A, given the belief X that the objective chance of A equals x, should equal x, no matter what other beliefs E one accepts. By this standard, every other belief has to be rationally irrelevant in arriving at the appropriate subjective probability.

Salmon's position, however, divides the inferential situation into (at least) two steps, the first of which involves an inference to a propensity:

(Step 1)   If z has observed that m/n Rs have been As, then z should infer that the propensity for any R to be $A = m/n$.

The second step is to use the conclusion of that inference as a premise to draw an inference about the particular instance of R under consideration:

(Step 2)   If z believes that the propensity for any R to be $A = m/n$, then z's degree of belief that this R is A should also $= m/n$.

Salmon thus provides a rather appealing account of the fashion in which frequencies, propensities, and personal probabilities ought to be related.

The other steps that Salmon considers involve the use of conditionalization to adjust inferences about propensity hypotheses with the accumulation of additional frequency evidence. His discussion reviews various notions of coherence, strict coherence, and openmindedness within a Bayesian framework that, in contrast with Lewis's account, is intended to provide an objective foundation for rational credibility. The most fascinating feature of this discussion, however, is the introduction of principles of reasoning about propensities as counterparts to the straight rule and Skyrm's Rule S, which have usually been employed within alternative frameworks.

Perhaps it should be emphasized that objective Bayesianism has some tremendous advantages over subjective Bayesianism as an access route to understanding science. Lewis' Principle Principle, after all, can be viewed as a special case of Carnap's requirement of total evidence, which depends on taking into account all of the available relevant evidence. Yet even if Lewis were completely successful in offering an account of how we ought to proceed in the formulation of *degrees of belief about events* as an epistemic enterprise, that would not mean he had provided an account about *objective chances* as an ontic conception. If we want to understand objective probabilities, we are going to have to study frequencies and propensities, not personal probabilities, even if they are related as Lewis suggests.

PROBABILITY AS A GUIDE IN LIFE

It is possible to have "probabilistic beliefs," however, that are not personal probabilities. An exploration of simple decision making indicates that rational decisions benefit from knowledge or information about objective probabilities to serve as our guide in life.

Indeed, this raises an important point that is widely overlooked, namely: there is a profound ambiguity in the phrase "probabilistic beliefs," because *probabilistic beliefs* in one sense are simply personal probabilities, but in another sense they are beliefs about objective chances instead. To appreciate this point, observe that, in order for a set of beliefs of a person to qualify properly as "rational," they must satisfy certain conditions that are necessary and sufficient for *rational belief.* Conditions that might be appropriate for this purpose include deductive closure, logical consistency, partial evidence, and complete evidence requirements (Fetzer 1981, Ch. 1).

While these conditions appear to be suitable whether the objects of belief happen to be deterministic hypotheses (concerning laws of universal strength, for example) or indeterministic hypotheses (concerning laws of probabilistic strength, for example), these beliefs could be held without having any beliefs that satisfy the personal conception of "degrees of belief." If you have any doubts on this score, simply consider the schemes for (U-D) and for (U-P) explanations within the context of the causal-relevance conception. Surely corresponding beliefs about premises such as these and the logical relations between them do not require "degrees of belief." Ordinary beliefs about expectations can function in their place.

In the case of personal probabilities, however, in order for some set of beliefs of a person to qualify properly as "rational," they must satisfy certain rather more specific conditions that are necessary and sufficient for *rational belief.* Conditions that might be appropriate for this purpose include coherence, strict coherence, and conditionalization (Salmon 1988, among many others, discusses these conditions). These are all possible counterparts to the conditions previously mentioned, but they differ by interpreting beliefs about expectations, which might otherwise be understood as ordinary beliefs about objective expectations, as subjective degrees of belief, which are understood instead as measures of credibility.

If Ginger, for example, happens to believe that the nomic expectability for Sally to recover, under the specific conditions of her illness, $= .1$, then she holds a belief that is either true or false about the nomic expectability for Sally to recover. If .1 is the nomic expectability for Sally's recovery under those conditions, then Ginger's belief is true and otherwise is false. Interpreted as a degree of belief, however, the only question of truth that arises is whether Ginger has the degree of belief $= .1$ that Sally will recover as one of her properties and not whether that belief corresponds to any objective properties of the world. The question of whether that belief bears some relation to the world does not even have to arise!

These differences notwithstanding, let us assume the existence of persons (not unlike ourselves) with motives and beliefs. While our behavior may be brought about by the complex interaction of motives, beliefs, ethics, abilities, capabilities, and opportunities (Fetzer 1991a), decision theory tends to be dominated by (almost) exclusive focus on beliefs and motives as determinants of decisions. The situation may be viewed as another instance of counterfactual idealization, which renders complex phenomena more easily tractable. In this instance, however, there may be greater justification, because decision theory is normative rather than descriptive.

The normative character of decision theory means that the questions that it addresses have to do with what a person (called an "agent") ought to do (in choosing a "course of action") when confronted by certain kinds of situations (involving possible "states of nature") in relation to the possible outcomes of those decisions and their values (known as "payoffs"). The alternative *courses of action* are assumed to be mutually exclusive and jointly exhaustive, while the *states of nature* are supposed to represent the mutually exclusive and jointly exhaustive range of situations an agent might encounter. The theory of decision examines and evaluates principles for making decisions in conditions like these (Michalos 1969).

Traditionally, three kinds of situation are distinguished depending on the kind of knowledge an agent happens to possess. If an agent knows the state of nature (how things are), decisions are being made under *conditions of certainty*. If the agent does not know the state of nature (how things are), decisions are being made under *conditions of uncertainty*. If the agent knows enough to assign probabilities to every possible state of nature, decisions are being made under *conditions of risk*. The theory of decision has become very complex, however, and we shall not pursue it very far. (As appropriate illustrations, cf. Jeffrey 1965 and Eells 1982.)

Some principles of decision do not require quantitative information about the probabilities of alternative outcomes, but (almost) every principle of decision requires knowledge of preferences between alternative payoffs. In order to illustrate some simple decision-making principles, consider an all too familiar situation encountered by members of both sexes: the offer of a blind date. We assume the following information:

States of Nature

Action Options	*He/She is wonderful*	*He/She is not wonderful*
Accept the date	Have a great time * * * *	Have a terrible time *
Reject the date	Miss a great time * *	Avoid a terrible time * * *

Figure 7. A Payoff Matrix

The situation is oversimplified, no doubt, but it will do. The general idea is that if you select one of the action options, then the payoff that you received depends upon the state of nature. If you accept the date and he/she is wonderful, for example, then you will have a great time, and so on.

Among the many principles that we might consider, certain qualitative principles are of special interest. These are known as the "minimax loss" and as the "maximax gain" principles and might be formulated as follows:

(DP-1) *the minimax loss principle*: adopt the course of action whose maximum loss is less than (or at least not greater than) that of any alternative;

(DP-2) *the maximax gain principle*: adopt the course of action whose maximum gain is greater than (or at least not less than) that of any alternative.

Informally expressed, the minimax loss principle advised you to minimize your losses, but the maximax gain principle advises maximizing your gains.

Neither principle, however, can be applied, even to our sample payoff matrix, until an (at least partial) ordering relation has been established between the possible payoffs. Suppose, for example, that we would prefer to have a great time over avoiding a terrible time over missing a great time over having a miserable time. Then the asterisks attached to the payoffs in Figure 7 indicate our relative preferences, where we prefer a four star payoff to a three star payoff, and so forth. Then it should be easy to see that we cannot simultaneously satisfy the advice generated by our rules, since minimax loss says "Reject the date" but maximax gain says "Accept." As you can see, the first is a policy for pessimists, the second for optimists.

So far as I have been able to discern, optimists are not inherently any more rational about making decisions than pessimists: it just depends on the kind of person you happen to be. Whatever the respective merits of these qualitative principles, a specific quantitative principle (sometimes known as "Bayes' Rule" as opposed to "Bayes' Theorem") has won considerable attention as perhaps the most promising general decision principle within situations characterized by information concerning probabilities:

(DP-3)   *maximize expected utility*: adopt that course of action whose expected utility is greater than (or not exceeded by) that of any alternative.

The application of this principle requires calculating the expected utility of each action option as follows. First determine the expected utility for each payoff as the product of the probability of that outcome times its utility. Then determine the sum of those expected utilities and select the action option for which the sum of those expected utilities is the greatest. This principle presupposes that each of these has a quantitative measure, which, in the case of the utilities, might be in terms of monetary benefits but might also be in terms of casualties lost (votes garnered, and so forth). While these considerations are fascinating, their consideration in greater detail would draw us away from the principal matters of relevance here.

Three general observations. First, sound decisions presume accurate beliefs about the probabilities of possible states of nature as well as suitable appraisals of the utilities of different outcomes. Personal probabilities, however, may be based upon information concerning frequencies, propensities, or other personal probabilities. Unless they are (directly or indirectly) based upon frequencies or propensities, they are merely subjective opinions without any objective foundation. Surely actions taken in the world should be based upon information about the world, a point that is important enough to be pursued in the following chapter.

Second, decision-theoretical accounts of rationality differ from dispositional accounts, because the normative character of principles of decision entails their inapplicability for the descriptive explanation of behavior, except when those principles have been assimilated as dispositions toward behavior. Thus, "reasons" can qualify as "causes" of behavior when they are causally-relevant features of explanation situations (cf. M. Salmon 1989 and Fetzer 1991a). Adequate explanations of behavior must still satisfy each of the appropriate conditions.

Third, optimizing principles of decision, such as that of maximizing expected utility, place tremendous emphasis upon choosing those acts whose expected utilities are not exceeded by those of *any* alternative. The proposal has been advanced by Herbert Simon, among others, however, that a more reasonable account of rational decision making may result from replacing the goal of "maximizing" with that of "satisficing," where *satisficing*, unlike *maximizing*, involves selecting action options that are "good enough" instead. (See Simon 1957 and Michalos 1973).

Although we have discovered that decision making would appear to benefit from knowledge or information about objective probabilities, decisions can be made on the basis of subjective probabilities, whether or not they are based upon objective probabilities.

CHAPTER SIX

THE PROBLEM OF INDUCTION

The problem of induction can be solved only if there are suitable grounds for the rational belief that the future will resemble the past. The solution appears to require a theory of the nature of laws of nature that Hume would have found to be unacceptable.

VALIDATION, VINDICATION, AND EXONERATION

In order to understand the problem, however, it is important to distinguish three different varieties of justification, namely: validation, vindication, and exoneration, and the characteristics that distinguish inductive reasoning from deductive reasoning.

Even though our primary attention has focused on approaches toward understanding science that embrace the frequency or the propensity conceptions of probability, it now appears as though the personal approach offers us another conception. During our discussion of these alternatives, significant distinctions among them have emerged. On the basis of each of these conceptions, for example, different visions of the motivating goal of science can be constructed, where each of these ideas about the aim of science can be complemented by further views about the methods appropriate to those aims. Most importantly, these differences are profound.

The personal perspective, for example, strongly hints that the aim of science might be that of maximizing expected utility. Since different persons have different motives and beliefs, however, this goal had better be envisioned as that of fostering each individual's capacity for maximizing his or her expected utility. The purpose of science, from this point of view, is to promote decision making by providing the resources that are required to *determine expectations*. Since rational decision making is based upon calculations of expected utilities, where different persons have their own motives and beliefs, this approach may or may not involve any essential reliance upon objective chance in the form of frequencies or propensities.

The frequency perspective, by contrast, suggests equally strongly that the aim of science should be the discovery of *objective frequencies*, where distinctions could be drawn between homogeneous and inhomogeneous reference classes, and the like. Frequencies might be appropriate for the purpose of prediction, moreover, whether or not they are suitable for the purpose of explanation. The straight rule of induction, for example, might be combined with Skyrms' Rule S to support determinations of objective expectations, which could be relied upon in arriving at calculations of expected utilities, when they are applied within decision-making contexts.

The propensity perspective suggests that the aim of science should be that of discovering *permanent properties* and universal and probabilistic strength dispositions, where corresponding laws could be invoked for the purposes of explanation and prediction. Indeed, the discovery of single-case propensities that are permanent properties of different chance setups affords a foundation for determining expectations for trial sequences of various lengths, whether infinite, finite, or singular. These expectations, in turn, could provide the source of another kind of information that might be employed in arriving at corresponding calculations of expected utilities, when they are applied within decision-making contexts.

Each of these conceptions of the aim of science has its own distinctive virtues. Surely the objective of supporting sound decision making seems to be praiseworthy. Surely the objective of discovering objective frequencies deserves to be endorsed. Surely the objective of discovering permanent properties and dispositions of universal and probabilistic strength is also an admirable goal. The questions that arise when confronted with these alternatives thus appear to be, first, whether there are means adequate to attain those objectives, and, second, whether one of them ought to be preferred over the others as a conception of the objective of science.

These questions appear to be appropriate with respect to the general distinctions that can be drawn concerning modes of justification. Herbert Feigl (1963), for example, separated "validation" from "vindication." An argument can be *validated* by establishing that it satisfies the accepted rules of reasoning for arguments of that kind. A rule of reasoning, however, can be *vindicated* by showing that it serves the purpose for which it was constructed. At least one more kind of justification should also be added to this list, however, because the purpose that a rule is intended to fulfill may need to be *exonerated* by showing that it is not unattainable.

The domains of deduction and of induction not only consist of sets of rules of reasoning and of sets of arguments that satisfy those rules but also have a program that they are intended to fulfill, which can be envisioned as their intended purpose. The aim of deduction from this point of view is to establish principles that are truth-preserving, while the aim of induction seems to be to establish principles that are knowledge-expanding. The exoneration of deduction consists in establishing that truth-preserving rules of reasoning are possible and showing how they can be constructed. A similar process might exonerate induction.

The problem confronting science that may not confront other activities is that there are different conceptions of its program. We have already discovered three of them, because the personal, the frequency, and the propensity approaches support different interpretations of the program that science should be envisioned as aiming to fulfill. If the aim of science is to foster decision making (to discover objective probabilities, or to discover permanent properties and such), then personal probabilities (objective frequencies, or single-case propensities) would seem to have the most important role to play within scientific contexts.

Since these are the alternatives, the purpose of this chapter is to evaluate the respective conceptions of the aim and methods of science that are supported by these approaches. The position I shall present maintains that, even though personal probabilities are sufficient for making decisions, those decisions are more appropriate when they are based upon objective probabilities. Even though objective frequencies are sufficient for forming predictions, those predictions are more appropriate when they are based on permanent properties and dispositions of universal and probabilistic strength. Only the propensity approach can supply principles suitable for explanation, prediction, and decision.

Before turning to this inquiry, however, it might be worthwhile to review the properties that distinguish inductive from deductive reasoning, which are three in number. Deductive reasoning is demonstrative, nonampliative, and additive, while inductive reasoning is nondemonstrative, ampliative, and nonadditive. Deduction is *demonstrative* because the conclusion of a (good) deductive argument cannot be false when its premises are true. Induction is *ampliative* because there is more content in the conclusion of a (good) inductive argument than is found in its premises. Arguments that are demonstrative, therefore, cannot be inductive and those that are ampliative cannot be deductive.

(Good) deductive arguments are *additive* in the sense that the addition of other premises to those arguments will not make them any less strong. (They are already "maximally strong.") (Good) inductive arguments, however, are nonadditive because the addition of further content in the form of additional premises can make them stronger or weaker. This is the reason that inductive arguments must satisfy the requirement of total evidence, which (you may recall) insists that any (good) inductive argument must be based, not on all the available evidence, but upon all the *relevant* evidence that is currently available.

Finally, (good) deductive arguments can be said to be "conclusive," while (good) inductive arguments are always "inconclusive." When an argument is such that its conclusion cannot be false when its premises are true, it is said to be *valid*. Valid arguments with true premises are said to be *sound*. An inductive argument that inconclusively supports its conclusion may be said to be *proper*. And a proper argument with true premises may be said to be *correct*.

Although a sound deductive argument cannot possibly have a false conclusion, the conclusion of an inductive argument can be false, even when it happens to be correct!

Whether an argument is intended to be deductive or inductive thus turns out to be an important question since, without knowing which, it would be difficult to determine the standards by means of which it should be appraised. Fortunately, different *conclusion indicators* that occur in ordinary language usually suffice to advise us. Phrases such as "consequently," "therefore," and "it follows that" are typical indications that an argument is intended to be deductive, while phrases such as "probably," "possibly," and "makes it likely that" are ordinarily inductive indicators.

RATIONALITY, MORALITY, AND DECISION

The necessity to base decisions on knowledge or information about objective probabilities emerges from considerations of the ethics of belief, according to which we are morally entitled to accept a belief only if we are logically entitled to accept that belief.

Each of the alternative conceptions of science that we have encountered might therefore be appraised from the perspective of validation, vindication, and exoneration. If the program of decision making can be exonerated on personalist principles and if personalist procedures can be vindicated as suitable for attaining that objective, then it will have been shown to be a viable conception of the nature of science. In order to provide the most favorable conditions for appraising the personalist approach, we should (hypothetically) disregard our prior investigation of science as devoted to the discovery of laws of nature.

The personalist approach to decision making, bear in mind, is a normative theory about how decisions ought to be made and not a descriptive theory for explaining how we do behave. It advances an account of the nature of rational action that presupposes a particular conception of the nature of rational belief. Thus, the sets of beliefs that are held by an "ideal agent" of this kind are envisioned as satisfying corresponding constraints of consistency and of closure (for beliefs about probabilities) or of coherence and of conditionalization (for degrees of belief) (Kyburg 1978 and Bacchus et al. 1990).

The simplest model of the personalist approach would assume the existence of degrees of belief rather than of beliefs about probabilities, with the added assumption that an *ideal agent* of the kind under consideration always makes decisions on the basis of the principle of maximizing utilities. Let us also assume that such an agent possesses complete awareness of his preferences and of his preferences among his preferences, so that an (at least partial) ordering of his relative preferences among alternative expected utilities poses no problems. Then the only element missing is a commitment to specific degrees of belief.

The "pure" personalist position would maintain that only subjective degrees of belief are necessary for making decisions within the context of this model because, whatever the evidential foundation upon which they might be based, "We have to use what we have to use in making decisions" (Eells 1993). But while rationality of belief on personalist principles only requires coherence and its complements, none of these conditions requires information about the world for their satisfaction. So long as an ideal agent's degrees of belief satisfy the requirements of the principles of probability, he can be "mad as a hatter" and still qualify as a rational thinker within the constraints imposed by such a model.

The problem can be exhibited by observing that, on purely personalist principles, anyone is entitled to hold any belief about anything (such as his own name, the date of the month, the state of the world, and so on) provided those beliefs cohere ("hang together") in an appropriate fashion. Moreover, absent conditionalization, any two agents at any one time and any one agent at any two times is entitled to completely different beliefs. The function of conditionalization, therefore, is to enforce a kind of consistency across time, where successive degrees of belief are supposed to be related to previous degrees of belief in conformity with Bayes' theorem. This, however, turns out to be a liberal requirement (Kyburg 1970, pp. 69–70).

Thus, on purely personalist principles, there need be no connection at all between objective probabilities (frequencies or propensities) and personal probabilities. Personalists can ignore objective probabilities if they choose, and no one, I presume, would suppose that personal probabilities alone provide suitable support for inferences to frequencies. A rule corresponding to Salmon's "Step 1," for example, could be formed as follows:

(Rule 1)   *Personal to Frequency*: If z's degree of belief that any R is an $A = m/n$, then z should infer that about m/n Rs are As.

This rule supports inferences from premises about subjective opinions to conclusions about objective frequencies. It is a wholly unjustifiable rule.

Since the conclusions of inferences in accordance with (Rule 1) could obviously be false when their premises were true (there is no conclusive connection between them), this cannot possibly be a valid principle of deduction. Although the content of its conclusions (which concern states of the world) obviously contain more content than do the premises (which concern states of mind), it must be an inductive principle, but it is surely not a proper one. That z happens to hold a degree of belief does not show that it is justified in even those specific cases toward which it is directed, much less for the classes of things that are corresponding generalizations.

Likewise, no one, I assume, would suppose that personal probabilities alone provide suitable support for inferences to propensities. A different rule corresponding to Salmon's "Step 1" could also be fashioned as follows:

(Rule 2)   *Personal to Propensity*: If z's degree of belief that any R is $A = m/n$, then z should infer that the propensity for any R to be an $A = m/n$.

This rule supports inferences from premises about subjective opinions to conclusions about single-case propensities. It too is a wholly unjustifiable rule. Indeed, since the conclusions of inferences in accordance with (Rule 2) have more content than do those obtained in accordance with (Rule 1), the same considerations as before count against the acceptability of a rule of this kind. It is not deductively valid, and it is not inductively proper.

The pure personalist position, however, does not depend upon links to objective probabilities for its adequacy. It could still be maintained, for example, that independence of subjective opinion from objective evidence does nothing to diminish the potential for ideal agents of this kind to make decisions, which are "rational" in conformity with pure personalist conditions. And, indeed, the problem with this position appears to be a question of morality rather than a question of epistemology. For such a position violates *the ethics of belief*, according to which you are morally entitled to hold a belief only if you are logically entitled to hold that belief (Clifford 1879). The problems with pure personalism are ethical.

It may already have occurred to you that, since pure personalists require no premises concerning objective probabilities in forming their degrees of belief, which in turn imply no conclusions concerning objective probabilities, "ideal agents" on pure personalist principles do not have to have any *evidence* whatever in support of their degrees of belief! The lunatic (of Bertrand Russell's creation) who thinks he is a poached egg may be just as "rational" as Albert Einstein in the sense of "rationality" that purely personalist principles support. Without evidence about objective probabilities, however, their degrees of belief are not justified!

The deep rationale for the ethics of belief is that we act on the basis of our beliefs and our actions tend to have consequences for others as well as ourselves. Decisions are rational only if they are based upon rational degrees of belief (or beliefs). The pure personalist conception of decision making agrees that decisions are rational only if they are based upon rational degrees of belief (or beliefs). But those degrees of belief (or beliefs) do not have to have (inductive or deductive) support from *evidence* about objective probabilities! The pure personalist conception appeals to a weak sense of "rational belief" that is morally indefensible.

The more serious the consequences the greater the obligation to insure that decisions are being made on the basis of all the relevant available evidence. Even simple choices can be poor decisions in the absence of objective knowledge. Bayer Aspirin costs $9.26 for 300 tablets, while generic aspirin runs $5.99 for 1000. Should you buy the name brand? (They are chemically the same!) Pinivil and Zestral are blood pressure medications with the same active ingredients that are sold for the same price. Does it matter which one you use? (They seem interchangeable, yet Zestral has an added dye that may bring about an allergic reaction.)

The decisions reached by an ideal agent of this kind who consults his personal preferences and degrees of belief without consulting the world would surely lead to sound decisions only by fortuitous coincidence. Unless they are (directly or indirectly) based on frequencies or propensities, his degrees of belief are subjective opinions without any objective foundation. Rational actions based on technically "rational" but morally irresponsible beliefs afford no expectation for successful results, other than by mere luck. An account of this kind could never vindicate the conception of science as directed toward the optimization of rational decisions.

FREQUENCIES AND MORE FREQUENCIES

Salmon has endorsed a pragmatic vindication of scientific method on the assumption that the aim of science is the discovery of limiting frequencies. While it appears to be successful as far as it goes, there are reasons for believing that we might be able to do better.

Acceptable solutions to problems tend to be bound by presuppositions about what kinds of proposals could qualify as acceptable. In the case of the problem of induction, for example, the classic version of the problem concerns inferences about the future on the basis of regularities that have obtained in the past. Some take for granted that any belief in necessary connections cannot be rationally warranted and therefore cannot figure in an acceptable solution. Others maintain that belief in necessary connections is not only rationally warranted but also essential to an acceptable solution. Still others contend (with considerable justification) that the very idea of a regularity requires further clarification before the problem can be solved.

Toward the end of the 1930s, Hans Reichenbach published a book that is remarkable for its clarity and verve (Reichenbach 1938). Reichenbach provided an astonishingly persuasive and beautifully argued case for the worldview of a Humean frequentist, complete with what has come to be known as a "pragmatic vindication" of induction within the framework of the frequency conception of objective probabilities. The tradition that he so forcefully represented has been perpetuated by Wesley C. Salmon, who was his student and who was profoundly affected by his influence. A nice example of Salmon's attempt to advance this worldview may be found in a recent article (Salmon 1975), written before he embraced propensities.

In the context of this paper, Salmon provides a highly engaging introduction to the problem from one who tends to side with Hume in rejecting belief in necessary connections as rationally unwarranted. As "Professor Philo" observes, what scientists mean by a "proof" of a law of nature is an exemplification of the law rather than a demonstration of its truth. Since laws are unrestrictedly general, their content cannot be exhausted by any finite number of tests. Discovering that specific observations and experiments satisfy a law, therefore, can only provide partial and inconclusive inductive evidence rather than complete and conclusive deductive proofs.

Moreover, that a specific regularity has obtained in the past provides no logical guarantee that it will continue to obtain in the future. Even if the conservation of momentum, for example, has been satisfied by every object in the past, that affords no guarantee that it will continue to hold in the future. Indeed, if there are no necessary connections between various events (or properties) in nature—that is, no logically contingent physical necessities—then it is entirely possible that *every prediction on the basis of any law might turn out to be false*. The consequences of denying the existence of natural necessities thus appear to be especially profound.

The solution that Salmon embraces assumes the form of what is called a *pragmatic vindication*, according to which the scientific method, were it pursued forever, supplies a suitable means for discovering uniformities in nature, provided that those uniformities exist to be discovered. If no such uniformities exist, of course, then they cannot be discovered by this or by any other means. Salmon admits that there are difficulties in developing an adequate conception of a natural law, but the general features of this approach are evident. If we want to pursue the discovery of natural laws, we have everything to gain and nothing to lose by using scientific method.

The argument can even be formulated by means of another payoff matrix, where "induction" is identified with the straight rule and "regularities" with limiting frequencies. The states of nature represent the existence or the non-existence of limits, while our options are to use induction or not:

	States of Nature	
Action Options	*Limits Exist*	*No Limits Exist*
Accept Induction	Discover those limits * * *	Discover no limits *
Reject Induction	Who knows? * *	Discover no limits *

Figure 8. A Pragmatic Vindication

When each possible payoff attending one action option equals or exceeds those of every other action option, that option may be said to "dominate" its alternatives. Reliance upon induction thus dominates its alternatives, since it is guaranteed to provide payoffs as good as or better than theirs.

The success of a pragmatic vindication of this kind crucially depends upon the identification of laws of nature and limiting frequencies together with the identification of scientific method and induction by enumeration by taking the straight rule and associated apparatus, such as Bayes' theorem, for example, as the method of science. What is appealing about this approach is its straightforward character. If the aim of science is to discover the limits of frequencies and if the method of science is induction by enumeration, then the method of science is guaranteed to achieve the aim of science, if any method can. No other method can make that claim.

There are some technical problems, of course. Since any relative frequency within any merely finite segment of an infinite sequence is logically compatible with any limit for that sequence, we can never be sure that we have discovered the limit of any sequence. That result, however, can be viewed as an aspect of the fallibility of inductive knowledge generally. Since few if any of those sequences that occur during the world's history are infinite rather than finite, and many of those of interest concern situations that might have no actual instances at all, these limits can even be viewed as counterfactual idealizations, as we discovered in Chapter Four.

We have already established the principal obstacles to the conception of laws as limiting frequencies and to the statistical-relevance model of explanation that attends it. We know that the requirement of objective homogeneity has proven exceedingly difficult, if not impossible, to formally define. We know that statistically relevant properties are not therefore explanatorily relevant. We know that "statistical explanations" can qualify as "statistical" only in the derivative sense supported by probabilities $= 0$ and $= 1$. Nevertheless, the bottom line regarding a pragmatic vindication of induction of this kind is, "Can we possibly do any better?"

Indeed, it is not difficult to establish that this approach offers more comparative benefits than the purely personal approach that we have reviewed. Principles of inference that relate frequencies and subjective probabilities, for example, are far more plausible than past alternatives:

(Rule 3)   *Frequency to Personal*: If z believes that m/n Rs are As, then z's degree of belief that any R is an A should $= m/n$.

On a "strict," purely personalist approach, this principle would not work, because there are no beliefs of the kind required by its antecedent. But we shall discover other grounds to reject the complete rejection of belief within the context of any conception of rationality in relation to science.

What is most appealing about (Rule 3), of course, is that it provides an objective foundation for the personal probabilities that may enter into the calculation of expected utilities in relation to which rational decisions might be made. Assuming that z's beliefs about frequencies result from the straight rule, this approach appears to overcome the primary objections that have been raised against the purely personal conception. The application of this rule in conjunction with the straight rule implies the satisfaction of the requirement of total evidence. Thus, the degrees of belief that result from its application are no longer merely subjective opinions with no objective foundation, which violate the ethics of belief.

A further rule that would permit inferences from frequencies to propensities and would be similar to Salmon's original may also be formed:

(Rule 4)   *Frequency to Propensity*: If z believes that m/n Rs are As, then z should infer that the propensity for any R to be an $A = m/n$.

Even when we assume that z's beliefs about frequences are invariably supported by inductive inferences from numerous observations obtained over a very wide variety of conditions, it should be obvious that the conclusion could be false even if such a premise were true. For example, think of accidental generalizations. Even if every Corvette the world has ever seen is red, this does not mean Corvettes have any such propensity.

Nevertheless, (Rule 4) clearly qualifies as a vastly preferable rule to some of its alternatives, such as (Rule 2), which would permit inferences to propensities on the basis of subjective opinions unsupported by any objective evidence. The question remains, "Can we possibly do better?", where the answer remains to be seen. In any case, the pragmatic vindication of scientific method provided by the frequency approach appears highly virtuous by comparison with the purely personal conception. An account of this kind even supplies evidence for the view that the results of science might contribute toward the optimization of rational decisions.

THE JUSTIFICATION OF INDUCTION

The discovery of limiting frequencies does not provide an adequate conception of the aim of science. When laws of nature are properly understood in terms of permanent property relations between dispositions, an adequate justification for induction becomes possible.

A suitable solution to the problem of induction appears to require a basic distinction between "permanent" and "transient" properties, where permanent properties are contingent dispositions something cannot lose without also losing a corresponding reference property. Dispositions are viewed in turn as single-case causal tendencies that may be of universal or of probabilistic strength. These conceptions provide an ontic foundation for fixing the truth conditions for subjunctive and for counterfactual conditionals. Lawlike sentences are true only when they are maximally specific and can be empirically tested by attempts to establish that they are false. The method of science is that of conjectures and refutations.

Since permanent properties are logically contingent attributes that cannot be taken away from something that has the corresponding reference property, they can be tested empirically by attempting to create or contrive situations in which those properties might be severed, if indeed they can be separated at all. When pure gold is defined by means of its atomic number, things that are pure gold have specific melting points and boiling points among their permanent properties. The permanence of those properties, however, can be tested empirically by attempting to separate those attributes from things that are pure gold, over and over.

Sentence functions that ascribe permanent properties are satisfied in all worlds that differ from the actual world, if at all, only with respect to their initial conditions, as Popper proposed. Hypotheses about permanent properties, therefore, can be subjected to experiments by efforts to create or contrive a world—*this world*—in which things with particular reference properties lack particular attributes. Observations and experiments can be employed to test the permanence of properties by means of sincere attempts to separate specific attributes from specific reference properties, where various attempts may be undertaken, again and again.

Salmon acknowledges that there appears to be a difference between the absence of material objects traveling faster than the speed of light and the absence of material objects that are enormous spheres of gold during the world's history. "The problem is," as Professor Philo remarks, "what basis do we have for claiming possibility in the one case and impossibility in the other?" If the speed of light imposes an upper bound on material objects (where it is impossible to travel faster and remain a material object), however, but things that are gold can be of any size and shape (while remaining things that are gold), then these differences in possibility may arise as a result of differences in permanent properties.

Hume's position, from this point of view, hinges upon the adoption of an epistemic principle that appears to be far too stringent to permit the rational belief in necessary connections, even if they exist. Their existence is not merely a matter of subjective expectation, moreover, since their presence or absence can be tested by attempting to violate them. The positive significance of unsuccessful attempts at refutation thus falls within the domain of inductive methodology, just as the negative significance of successful attempts at refutation falls within the domain of deductive methodology. The key to scientific method is attempts to falsify.

The success of induction in the discovery of natural laws thus depends upon our possession of a method that enables us to distinguish laws from non-laws. Even if all Corvettes are red (all my friends are rich, and so on), under suitable conditions, we can establish that those generalizations are not laws by discovering processes or procedures, natural or contrived, by means of which something with those attributes could lose them without also losing their possession of that reference property. If we discovered processes or procedures by means of which a Corvette could lose its redness while remaining a Corvette (by repainting it), then we would know that, even if all Corvettes were red, that generalization cannot be a law.

If this approach is right-headed, then the difference between law-like sentences and accidental generalizations is not precisely as Goodman implies. Accidental generalizations are expressible in extensional language and are capable of confirmation by their instances, sometimes by means of simple inductive methods, such as the straight rule of induction. Lawlike sentences are only expressible in intensional language and are tested by attempts to refute them. Goodman's resolution of the problem of law does not appear to be the best that we can do. The reason it has been so difficult to solve seems to be a consequence of mistakes in methodology.

Indeed, a fascinating illustration of Goodman's ultimate incapacity to come to grips with the question of what it means for a sentence to be lawlike can be found in his original paper on the problem of counterfactual conditionals, which receives its latest (partially revised) incarnation in Goodman (1983). A sentence that Goodman himself proposes as an example of a lawlike sentence is the generalization, "All dimes are silver" (Goodman 1983, p. 25). Even though this claim once seemed to be true, today dimes are minted from copper and silver. It was never lawlike. Yet in the past we accepted it as true and we projected it for unknown cases without having exhausted its instances, in violation of Goodman's thesis (T2).

This illustration thus provides an example of a previously true generalization that happens to be a *law of society* rather than a *law of nature*. Laws of societies must be passed by legislative bodies, interpreted by judiciary bodies, and enforced by executive bodies. I spoke with Goodman during a reception that followed a conference a number of years ago and chided him about his example, but he cleverly replied, "They changed the law!" As we—you and I and he—all know, however, while laws of society can be violated and changed, laws of nature cannot be violated or changed. When "they changed the law," they broadened the legal definition of "dime."

The differences between propensity-based and frequency-based solutions to the problem of induction affords an opportunity to explore some differences between Salmon's proposal for inferring from observed frequencies to propensities and something that ought to work a little better:

(Rule 5)   *Higher Induction*: If z has observed that *m/n* Rs have been As, then z should infer that the propensity for any R to be A = *m/n*.

Even if we make the assumptions that these observations are numerous and conducted over a wide range of conditions, this provides no reason to believe (Rule 5) will not yield merely accidental generalizations, such as that every dime that has been observed in New York (Chicago, and so on) during sunny days (rainy nights, and so on) has been made of silver.

The alternative approach—which reflects Popper's method—takes into account that accidental generalizations, unlike natural laws, can be violated and can be changed. The appropriate method to use thus depends upon repeated but sincere efforts to violate or to change that regularity:

(Rule 6)   *Corroboration*: if z has discovered that *m/n* Rs have been As, a claim that has resisted our best attempts to refute it, then z should infer that the propensity for any R to be an A = *m/n*.

Thus, the differences between (Rule 5) and (Rule 6)—presuming that our "best attempts" are both suitable and sincere—are precisely those that Popper has repeatedly emphasized, where the evidence that confirms a generalization does not necessarily support a law, unless it has been acquired under appropriate test conditions (Fetzer 1981, p. 201). Without corroboration, "higher induction" would possess no vindication.

THE FUNDAMENTAL QUESTION ABOUT CHANCE

The ultimate explanation for why we should base our expectations on objective probabilities rather than merely on subjective beliefs emerges at last. Laws of nature, unlike relative frequencies and personal probabilities, cannot be violated and cannot be changed.

Bas van Fraassen has introduced what he calls "the fundamental question about chance," which is, "How and why should beliefs about objective chance help to shape our expectations about what will happen?" (van Fraassen 1989, p. 81). While he maintains that this question is a generalization of the problem of discovering the values of chances, no one should take that claim very seriously. What van Fraassen has in mind is that the value of these values should be measured in relation to their contribution to the calculation of personal probabilities and the process of making decisions. Even if this is not "the fundamental question," it is still an important one.

We should therefore consider counterpart principles of inference for relating propensities to frequencies and to personal probabilities. Here is a rule that relates beliefs about propensities to beliefs about frequencies:

(Rule 7)   *Propensity to Frequency*: If z believes that the propensity for an R to be an $A = m/n$, then z should infer that about m/n Rs are As.

Not "exactly," of course, but it would be the case that, as the length of the sequence of trials becomes increasingly longer, the tendency for the relative frequency to approximate the strength of the propensity becomes increasingly stronger, even without any guarantees (Fetzer 1981, Ch. 9).

And a rule relating beliefs about propensities to personal probabilities in the form of degrees of belief could similarly be formulated as follows:

(Rule 8)   *Propensity to Personal*: If z believes that the propensity for any R to be an $A = m/n$, then z's degree of belief that any R is an A should $= m/n$.

The benefit of this principle over its frequency counterpart is that, while they both provide an objective foundation for personal probabilities that should enter into the calculation of expected utilities in relation to which rational decisions might be made, (Rule 8), unlike

(Rule 3), supports inferences based upon (beliefs about) regularities that have the status of laws of nature. Thus, on the assumption that z's beliefs about propensities result from the application of procedures appropriate for discovering laws, this principle supplies a stronger objective foundation for rational decisions.

The problem that van Fraassen raises reflects the gap between actual frequencies that occur during the course of the world's history and the objective chances that may obtain as features of the world's structure. These actual frequencies cannot be natural laws, which is clear, yet those objective chances cannot guarantee actual frequencies, which creates a tension between them. Since objective chances, at best, can guarantee the limits of frequencies in infinite sequences but no relative frequencies or singular events, van Fraassen claims, we have no reason to base our personal opinions and subjective expectations about the course of events upon them.

The reason why we should base our subjective expectations on physical propensities, when they are known, is that, as properties of laws of nature, these propensities cannot be violated and cannot be changed. Admittedly, the problems involved in discovering propensity values can be formidable, indeed; but consider the alternative. If our subjective expectations about actual frequencies in the future are instead based, not upon natural laws, but upon actual frequencies in the past, there is no good reason to believe that they cannot be violated or that they cannot be changed. And if our subjective expectations are based neither on objective chances nor on actual frequencies, the only alternative that remains appears to be (other) personal opinions. And that would obviously violate the ethics of belief.

When the aim of science is cast broadly enough to include explanations that are adequate, the limitations of the personalist approach become even more obvious. The construction of adequate explanations—no matter whether those are simple "nomic" explanations, causal-relevance explanations, or theoretical explanations—clearly depends upon the availability of appropriate premises that may serve as the explanans of those very explanations. If explanations are arguments, then their assertion as adequate entails their acceptance as true. Insofar as science aims at explanation, therefore, it cannot dispense with acceptance (Fetzer 1981, p. 246). Conceptions of science require *probabilistic beliefs* rather than *degrees of belief* to be acceptable.

It could be maintained, no doubt, that "degrees of belief" are necessary to rational decision making, even if they are not sufficient. Perhaps when they are based upon objective probabilities, preferably about propensities but possibly about frequencies, they continue to qualify as elements that are essential to a complete account of science. If we can have probabilistic beliefs about degrees of nomic expectability, however, as our previous considerations suggest, then even this rationale for the personal approach cannot be defended. Thus, the personal appeal to "degrees of belief" does not appear to be necessary or sufficient to an adequate account of science.

What then about the frequency conception? Surely the discovery of frequencies by means of simple inductive methods ought to qualify as elements that are essential to an adequate account of science. And there does appear to be ground for adopting this position, since the discovery of frequencies appears to be necessary for the discovery of laws, even if it cannot qualify as sufficient. Indeed, in an absence of knowledge of laws about propensities, knowledge about frequencies would appear to afford a far preferable foundation for rational decision making than mere subjective opinion. Science can supply explanations that are adequate, however, only if it has the capacity to acquire knowledge of laws of nature.

The discovery of natural laws thus exceeds those epistemic resources that Hume would permit, a fateful blunder that has affected the history of philosophy ever since. For Hume insisted that every justifiable idea has to be reducible to impressions from experience and *deductive* consequences that follow from them. But he should have insisted instead that justifiable ideas only have to be reducible to impressions from experience and *inductive* consequences that follow from them. A more liberal conception would support inferences about natural laws, even though our knowledge of those laws must always be uncertain as a product of fallible inductive reasoning.

Indeed, that Hume's position cannot be sustained becomes clear in relation to the following reconstruction of his critique of necessary connections:

Necessary connections between events are either observable and objective or psychological and subjective. But they cannot be ascertained on the basis of experiential considerations alone. Consequently, they must be merely psychological and subjective. (Fetzer 1981, p. 198)

The premise that necessary connections must be *either* observable and objective *or* psychological and subjective thereby poses a misleading dilemma. This crucial assumption precludes the possibility that necessary connections, as theoretical properties of the world, might be unobservable and *nevertheless* objective, which could be tested by sincerely attempting to refute them.

The general conception of science that emerges from these considerations at last, therefore, is that science endeavors to fulfill at least two complementary objectives: first, to ascertain the frequency patterns displayed by the world's history; and, second, to discover the lawful relations constitutive of the world's structure. The solution to the problem of induction is that, even if the world is as we believe it to be with respect to the laws of nature, it is *logically possible* that the future might not resemble the past in those very respects; but if the world is as we believe it to be with respect to the laws of nature, it is not *physically possible* that the future will not resemble the past in those very respects. So induction appears to be justifiable, after all.

Hume imposes an excessive standard in limiting acceptable inferences to impressions from experience and their deductive consequences. Laws of nature that cannot be violated and cannot be changed are respects in which the future must resemble the past.

CHAPTER SEVEN

THE GROWTH OF SCIENTIFIC KNOWLEDGE

The growth of scientific knowledge appears to be a process of conjectures and (attempted) refutations. This Popperian conception, however, has been challenged by Kuhn and by Lakatos on widely differing grounds, which invites us to consider the matter further.

CONJECTURES AND REFUTATIONS

The problem of demarcation is that of discovering a suitable criterion for distinguishing science from nonscience. Popper offers the principle of empiricism and suggests how it can be applied to the tentative acceptance of probabilistic scientific hypotheses.

While the authors we have studied up to now have tended to emphasize the products of science as opposed to the process of science, others have focused their attention upon the history of science as a guide to the philosophy of science. Upon initial consideration, after all, it seems enormously promising to suppose that the questions we have been considering might be settled by the study of the history of science, where the actual practice of scientists could provide a basis for arbitrating between conflicting conceptions. Thus, the normative questions that have preoccupied philosophers might be amenable to descriptive solutions by increased sensitivity to the historical record.

Popper (1968, pp. 33–65) devotes attention to the *problem of demarcation*, which attempts to separate science from nonscience, as opposed to the *problem of meaningfulness*, which attempts to distinguish sense from nonsense. In the process of elaborating the virtues of his falsificationist methodology, he discusses various theories of the past, including the dialectical materialism of Marx, the psychoanalytic theory of Freud, and the individual psychology of Adler. These "theories," however, do not fare well in comparison to other theories, such as the theory of relativity of Einstein, because the former, unlike the latter, appear to be compatible with virtually any possible outcome.

Popper emphasizes what he takes to be the crucial characteristics of scientific theories, which assert prohibitions about the world's behavior. The more a theory prohibits, the greater its content and the greater its testability. As a result, "A theory that is not refutable by any conceivable event is non-scientific." Every genuine test of a theory is an effort to falsify or to refute it, where apparently confirming evidence does not properly count as supporting a theory except when it results from a sincere attempt to falsify or to refute it. The findings supplied by inductive confirmations, therefore, should not be mistaken for the evidence provided by attempted refutations.

Although many religious beliefs appear to violate Popper's requirement, this may render them *nonscientific*, but it does not make them *meaningless*. Indeed, the Popperian criterion of demarcation must be understood to have a very different objective than those criteria of cognitive significance that were intended to separate "sense" from "nonsense" (especially, Ayer 1949). The repeated failure of successive attempts to capture such a distinction by means of formal criteria, which Hempel (1965, pp. 101–122) has so lucidly reviewed, therefore, has nothing to do with Popper's criterion as a means for distinguishing scientific from nonscientific deliberations and discourse.

The difference involved is easily illustrated by articles of religious faith. The belief, "God brings all things to pass," for example, may not satisfy this condition, because its truth appears to be compatible with the history of the world no matter what its course. The occurrence of plagues, pestilence, and famine may not disconfirm or falsify this hypothesis, because it can simply be God's will that plagues, pestilence, and famine should occur. Unless we have direct or indirect access to the mind of God on the basis of empirical evidence, we have no idea what God has in mind. Events like these might test a believer's faith in God when conceived as an omniscient, omnipotent, and benevolent being, but they cannot function as tests of that hypothesis.

Of course, as a general rule, neither articles of religious faith nor scientific hypotheses can be properly appraised without unpacking their meaning. Beliefs about God, like those about gravity, might be true or might be false under different interpretations. According to pantheism, God and nature are one and the same, while according to polytheism, there are many gods. According to pantheism, evidence for the existence of nature would also count as evidence for the existence of God, but not on other accounts. One of the lessons of the study of science appears to be that we have to understand the meaning of an hypothesis before we undertake to test it.

Without doubt, Popper's position is strongly deductivist. He maintains, "Only the falsity of a theory can be inferred from empirical evidence, and this inference is a purely deductive one" (Popper 1965, p. 55). As we have already discovered, however, a distinction must be drawn between "induction" in its *broad* and in its *narrow* senses. Popper may be on solid ground in rejecting the straight rule of induction or probabilistic measures of confirmation, but scientific inquiries would still remain ampliative. And even if decision making does not require the acceptance of any theories as true, the situation appears to be different with respect to scientific explanation.

A crucial point deserves to be mentioned again, namely: that while the negative significance of successful attempts at refutation fall within the domain of *deductive* methodology, the positive significance of unsuccessful attempts at refutation falls within the domain of *inductive* methodology instead (Fetzer 1981, p. 176). Once the difference between deduction as demonstrative and induction as ampliative has been adequately understood, it should be clear that science cannot succeed without the benefit of induction. The content of lawlike hypotheses always exceeds the content of our evidence. Science could not attain its aim without the benefit of induction.

In fact, Popper endorses what he calls a *principle of empiricism*, which asserts that, "in science, only observation and experiment may decide upon the *acceptance or rejection* of scientific statements, including laws and theories" (Popper 1965, p. 54, original emphasis). He thus embraces the idea that laws and theories are accepted and rejected, with the understanding that laws and theories may only be accepted as tentative conjectures that may subsequently be rejected on the basis of new evidence, even without discarding the old evidence that led us to accept them. But this is about as clear a formulation of the condition of total evidence as could be made.

The distinction between acceptance and rejection, no doubt, deserves additional elaboration. The situation with respect to statistical hypotheses is not the same as that for ordinary theories. Thus, for example, as we have learned, the existence of any limiting frequency over an infinite sequence is logically compatible with any relative frequency over a finite segment. But Popper recognized that, although arbitrary deviations from limiting values within (random) sequences were *logically possible*, they were not therefore *equally probable*. By exploiting the results of classic limit theorems of the calculus of probability, including Bernoulli's theorem, Popper extended his methodology to statistical hypotheses (Popper 1965).

The foundation for his extension was the adoption of a *supplementary principle* to the effect that, since almost all possible segments of large size will very probably exhibit relative frequencies that are very close to the limiting frequencies of these infinite sequences, outcomes that are highly improbable deserve systematic neglect (Popper 1965, pp. 410–419). He has thus sought to defend the position that the testing of statistical hypotheses, like that of all other scientific hypotheses, is basically deductive. The probabilities of various frequency distributions over large but finite samples are mathematically derived using the principles of the calculus of probability, highly improbable outcomes are supposed not to occur and the various hypotheses under consideration are confronted by experience.

Similar principles were introduced into the statistical literature by J. Neyman and E. Pearson in a form that is known as *orthodox statistical hypothesis testing*. In relation to the specification of the "significance level" of a statistical test, they drew a distinction between two kinds of mistakes that might be made as a result of the influence of chance (or randomness), which cannot be simultaneously maximized. The first kind (called "errors of Type I") consists of rejecting an hypothesis when it is true, while the second (called "errors of Type II") consists of accepting an hypothesis when it is false. The failure to reject an hypothesis at a specific significance level as the result of an empirical test, however, provides no guarantee that that hypothesis is true, precisely as Popper proposed (Fetzer 1981, pp. 234–244).

Although Popper elaborated these principles in relation to frequency hypotheses, they are also applicable to propensity hypotheses, provided they are implemented as severe tests within the framework of the theory of corroboration. This requires not only that a large number of trials be conducted under a wide variety of conditions, but also that the conditions that are most likely to "make a difference" to the attributes of interest must be systematically investigated. Propensity hypotheses can only be subjected to appropriate empirical tests when they are under conditions of this kind, which lends further weight to the analysis of inference rules in Chapter Six.

Surprising as it may appear, however, even lawlike hypotheses of universal strength can only be subjected to appropriate empirical tests in relation to a variety of related suppositions. These take the form of assumptions about the initial conditions, the background knowledge, and the auxiliary hypotheses that make a difference to the empirical testability of the hypotheses under consideration. Thus, no hypothesis or theory can be subjected to empirical test without making assumptions concerning conditions of each of these other kinds. Because this observation was first advanced by Pierre Duhem (1906), it is customarily referred to as *the Duhem thesis*.

NORMAL SCIENCE VS. REVOLUTIONARY SCIENCE

The greatest challenge to the Popperian conception of the growth of scientific knowledge has been advanced by Kuhn, who suggests that revolutionary science (of the kind Popper has described) is a relatively infrequent occurrence and that most science is different.

Kuhn has challenged Popper's conception of scientific method on historical grounds, contending that the history of science reflects a great deal of scientific activity that cannot be accurately described in falsificationist language (Kuhn 1962 and 1970a). Kuhn maintains that a fundamental distinction must be drawn between "normal science" and "revolutionary science," where Popper's conceptions, at best, characterize extraordinary events during revolutionary periods rather than the typical conduct of normal practice. Most scientists spend most of their time attempting to expand the power of widely accepted theories (or "paradigms") and are not trying to refute them.

Kuhn thus distinguishes between "problem solving" in a Popperian sense and "puzzle solving" in his sense, where *problem solving* involves establishing a paradigm, but *puzzle solving* involves extending an accepted paradigm. Although Popper considers critical discourse and severe testing as criteria of scientific activity, Kuhn considers the abandonment of criticism and the conduct of puzzle solving as typical of normal science. Even though Kuhn tends to agree with Popper's position as a description of revolutionary activities in science, he disagrees with Popper's position as a description of the ordinary activity of scientists. Most of scientific activity is normal, not revolutionary.

Their most striking differences emerge from the respective roles that they assign to logic and to psychology. Kuhn contends that normal science can be conducted even when confronted with "anomalies," phenomena that do not fit the accepted paradigm. Since anomalies are inconsistent with or otherwise contravene the adopted theory, they should qualify as falsifying instances that warrant its rejection, from the Popperian perspective. Kuhn contends that scientists will persist in attempting to extend their paradigms until they discover an alternative theory with the capacity to resolve a substantial proportion of accumulated anomalies without generating new ones.

The difficulty encountered at this juncture by Kuhn's conception is that it can easily give rise to the impression that changes in paradigm are more a matter of psychology than they are of logic. Indeed, if there is nothing more to truth in science than consensus among scientists, then it might be said that accepted theories are on a par with political ideologies and that paradigm changes are on a par with religious conversions. Kuhn takes for granted that the members of the scientific community have the right kind of background, education, and training. But this raises the further question of just what kind of background, education, and training is the right kind.

One mode of reconciliation between their divergent views is to consider them as complementary rather than competitive. Alan F. Chalmers (1976) has offered an illuminating indication of the benefits of *mixed strategies*:

It is a mistake to regard the falsification of bold, highly falsifiable conjectures as the occasion of significant advance in science. . . . Significant advances will be marked by the *confirmation* of *bold* conjectures and the *falsification* of *cautious* conjectures. . . . By contrast, little is learnt from the *falsification* of a *bold* conjecture or the *confirmation* of a *cautious* conjecture. (Chalmers 1976, pp. 51–52, original emphasis)

He elaborates on this theme by observing that the falsification of improbable conjectures (such as Kepler's theory of the solar system based on the five Platonic solids) and the confirmation of probable conjectures (such as that samples of iron extracted by a new process will expand when heated) do not count as especially significant contributions to the history of science.

These reflections, I believe, provide appropriate ingredients for a decision-theoretic comparison of these alternative methodologies on the basis of a payoff matrix that represents the epistemic utilities of success and failure employing different modes of inquiry under different research conditions:

Research Results

Mode of Inquiry	Confirmation	Falsification	Kuhnian Character
Bold Conjectures	* * * *	*	Revolutionary Science
Cautious Conjectures	* *	* * *	Normal Science

Figure 9. An Epistemic-Utility Payoff Matrix

For the purpose of this matrix, epistemic utilities are envisioned as contributions to the growth of scientific knowledge, where the number of asterisks that occur indicate the comparative utilities of the payoffs obtainable given various research outcomes that may attend these modes of inquiry.

Since the boldness of a conjecture may be measured by the extent to which its content exceeds (or contravenes) the content of accepted background knowledge, the investigation of cautious conjectures may be characteristic of *normal*, as opposed to *revolutionary*, science, in Kuhn's sense. Thus, scientists desiring some guarantee that their research might make more than a minimal contribution to the advance of science should adopt the *minimax loss* strategy and practice normal science. But scientists who prefer the possibility that their efforts might make maximal contributions to the growth of scientific knowledge should adopt the alternative *maximax gain* strategy and practice revolutionary science (Fetzer 1979, p. 401).

These considerations suggest that Kuhn's conception of a scientific community might be reconciled with the Popper's conception of scientific method by making Popperian training a condition for membership within such a Kuhnian community. The principal difficulty with this approach appears to be Kuhn's emphasis upon the *abandonment* of critical discourse as a feature that is essential to normal science. The commitment to its "paradigm" within a Kuhnian community is so profound that difficulties in solving puzzles that have not yet been resolved are attributed to the scientist's own shortcomings rather than to that paradigm's limitations. Normal science is a process that tests scientists rather than a process that tests theories.

Given Kuhn's conception, the growth of knowledge involves changes between paradigms. When this occurs, those who are trained within a puzzle-solving tradition will preserve as many of the puzzles that the community has successfully resolved and maximize the number that could be solved. But appeals to these properties may leave choices between competing paradigms, where considerations of simplicity, precision, and coherence might

not all dictate the same choice nor will they all be applied in the same way. That being the case, it is also important that group unanimity be a paramount value, causing the group to minimize the occasions for conflict and to reunite quickly about a single set of rules for puzzle solving even at the price of subdividing the specialty or excluding a formerly productive member. (Kuhn 1970a, p. 21)

Passages such as this one appear to leave open the possibility that science not only does not discover the truth about nature but cannot even be properly said to approach ever closer to the truth. This hints that the sociology of science might eventually displace the philosophy of science. But there is an important difference between popular practice and proper method.

We are going to discuss this question several times. It should be apparent, however, that Kuhn's conception of scientific procedure appears inadequate in relation to his conception of the aim of science. You might recall that the purpose of science, according to Kuhn, is the discovery of cosmologies, theories, or paradigms that are both psychologically satisfying and provide empirically testable explanations for observable phenomena. If the assertion of explanations implies their acceptance as true, then the aim of science can be attained only if the methods of science are conducive to the discovery of explanations that might possibly be true.

THE METHODOLOGY OF RESEARCH PROGRAMS

An alternative approach has been advanced by Lakatos, who holds that scientists tend to nurture "infant" theories by protecting them from falsification, supplying a conception of science where theories are retained in spite of refutation by observation and experiments.

In a remarkable study, Imre Lakatos (1971) has provided a survey of inductivism, conventionalism, falsificationism, and the methodology of research programs as alternative conceptions of the nature of science. He shares with Kuhn the conviction that scientists should persist in nurturing an infant theory by deflecting the falsifying significance of apparently incompatible findings ("anomalies") onto the background knowledge, the auxiliary hypotheses, and the initial conditions attending its obtainment. This approach thus incorporates

Duhem's view that, as a point of logic, theories are never subject to direct tests but only in combination with other claims.

The Duhem thesis can be illustrated by the historically important case of Galileo's observations of the Moon by means of a telescope of his own design. According to Aristotelian cosmology, a fundamental distinction is found in nature between "celestial" phenomena and "terrestrial" phenomena. Aristotle maintained that bodies of different kinds invariably move toward their natural place by means of natural motion, when they are not subject to force. The natural place of earth was supposed to be the center of the universe, of water above earth, and so on. The heavenly bodies traversed the heavens in uniform circular motion, which was perfect motion.

Another feature of Aristotle's conception was the thesis that heavenly bodies, in addition to exhibiting perfect motion, possess perfect spherical shapes. Thus, when Galileo turned his telescope toward the heavens and discovered a Moon with a pockmarked and irregular surface, he had located evidence that apparently disconfirmed or refuted Aristotle's theory. But the ecclesiastical authorities were in the position of rebutting Galileo's findings by maintaining either that his telescope was not working properly, that the object of his perception was not really the Moon, or that things that are spherical do not always look spherical, under various conditions.

In effect, these religious leaders, whose Christian faith had become inextricably intertwined with Aristotelian cosmology, were maintaining that the satisfaction of an hypothesis or theory is always attended by a *ceteris paribus* (or "other things being equal") clause that covers the additional conditions whose presence or absence make a difference to the outcome of an empirical test. In this case, they could maintain the truth of Aristotle's conception by deflecting the falsifying significance of an incompatible outcome onto the initial conditions ("He was not looking at the Moon"), the auxiliary hypotheses ("His telescope was not working properly"), or the background knowledge ("Things that are spherical do not look spherical under these specific conditions") attending its obtainment and thereby defend it.

The subtle hazard thereby generated, however, is that the methodology that protects the *hard core* of basic assumptions that constitute a theory by granting it temporary immunity by deflecting the falsifying significance of incompatible evidence onto the *protective belt* of auxiliary hypotheses, etc., has to specify how long "temporary immunity" should endure. Otherwise, the transition from Popperian principles to Lakatosian programs degenerates from a methodology emphasizing that the fate of theories has to be decided on the basis of experiments and observation to one that endorses "the conventionalist stratagem," whereby a theory is retained *in spite of* its experiential refutation. When, after all, should a theory be abandoned?

For Lakatos, the crucial measure of the scientific significance of alternative programs is a function of the extent to which their hard cores contribute to the discovery of novel phenomena (thereby qualifying as *progressive*, since they promote the growth of scientific knowledge, whereas those that do not are *degenerative* and therefore should be abandoned). Because future discoveries might revive an abandoned theory or undermine its successors, the progress of science is never conclusive. The shift from Popperian falsification to Kuhnian paradigms to Lakatosian programs thus ultimately leads to a theory where successes count but failures do not.

The most important aspect of this conception appears to be the extent to which its features cannot be completely understood from the perspective of the requirement of total evidence. If the hypotheses and theories which are established (however tentatively) by scientific inquiries are the product of an inductive process, it should not be surprising when they come and go as a function of the available relevant evidence. There are many reasons why hypotheses and theories might be highly supported by a body of evidence at one time and weakly supported by a body of evidence at some other. But the methodology of research programs goes beyond rules of inference by implying that the results of science should never be viewed as final and complete *and* that sometimes the reason might be subjective.

Perhaps the most valuable aspect of Lakatos' study is the difficulties it discloses for purely descriptive approaches. Each methodology yields a distinctive *internal history* as a rational reconstruction of the history of science from its point of view. Each of these normative interpretations will have to be supplemented by empirical *external histories* to account for the nonrational factors that affect the growth of science. In this sense, he maintains, "The history of science is always richer than its rational reconstructions." But rational reconstructions (or internal histories) are always primary and empirical descriptions (or external histories) are always secondary, where the role of external histories is to explain the anomalies of internal histories.

During his discussion of the methodologies of Popper, Kuhn, and Lakatos, Chalmers has noticed the extent to which subjective decisions figure as elements of scientific procedure on all of the methodologies under consideration. Popper emphasizes the importance of *individual decisions* in accepting and rejecting basic statements (which describe the contents of experience), Lakatos indicates the influence of *group decisions* in adopting and abandoning research programs (when they cease to be progressive), and Kuhn asserts the centrality of *community decisions* for retaining and discarding different paradigms (when other paradigms would do better).

In order to eradicate these vestiges of subjectivity, Chalmers endorses a conception of scientific knowledge as the practice of a complex activity based upon objective techniques (which might be mathematical, experimental, theoretical, or whatever), where the autonomous status of these practices "leaves room for the possibility of individual scientists or groups of scientists failing to carry out the practice adequately" (Chalmers 1976, p. 107). The difficulty here is that alchemy, astrology, and witchcraft, for example, are autonomously existing complex social activities whose practitioners could fail to carry them out, but therefore qualify as "sciences" no more than do mortuary science, library science, and Christian Science merely because they are so called. The difference surely lies elsewhere.

At a deeper level, however, it should be obvious that purely descriptive approaches to science are fundamentally misconceived. Historians cannot study the history of science without having some idea of which persons are scientists and which activities are scientific and why. "Science" could be defined as what the members of the presumptive community of scientists do only by taking for granted that they are not frauds, quacks, or incompetents. The possibility of malpractice guarantees that the principles and procedures by means of which a discipline is properly defined cannot be adequately ascertained by empirical methods alone. Indeed, "science" cannot be defined merely as what the members of the "scientific community" do. On the contrary, the members of the scientific community are those who do science.

INFERENCE TO THE BEST EXPLANATION

Inference to the best explanation can be properly understood as relating the theory of explanation to the theory of induction. Degrees of nomic expectability as logical probabilities establish the foundation for nomic inference via Hacking's Law of Likelihood.

We know that knowledge of natural laws arises from empirical procedures employing inductive reasoning and can never be certain or infallible. From this point of view, the most difficult task that science confronts is the problem of separating "good" guesses from "bad" guesses about the laws of nature. We know this process involves testing laws by attempting to refute them. By trying to show that a guess is wrong we possibly obtain evidence that a guess might be right. Such evidence is always inconclusive, because even if our guesses survive our best efforts to refute them, it does not show that they are correct. We may have not yet discovered how to refute them!

What we do not know is how to measure the degree of evidential support that specific evidence should confer on lawlike hypotheses within the framework of corroboration as a methodology. Since laws are employed especially for the purpose of explanation, inferences to laws may be appropriately envisioned as inference to explanations, in the sense that the law that provides the best explanation for the available relevant evidence appears most likely to be true. When alternative possible laws compete for acceptance, then the approach to employ would appear to be "inference to the best explanation," a pattern of reasoning that Gilbert Harman (1970), especially, has endorsed.

You may remember from Chapter Five that a probabilistic explanation for the occurrence of a singular event must assume the following logical form:

(U-P″) Probabilistic Law: $(x)(t)(Rxt =p\geqslant Axt^*)$
           Initial Conditions: Rat'
$$\overline{\hspace{3cm}}\,[p]$$
           Explanandum: Aat'^*

where [p] is the degree of nomic expectability that the explanans confers upon its explanandum, when the appropriate conditions of adequacy are satisfied. The value of [p] is determined by the value of p, but they possess very different meanings. The value of p is that of an *empirical probability* (that of a single-case propensity), where the value of [p] is that of a *logical probability* instead (that of a degree of nomic expectability).

One way to appreciate the difference between them is to notice that, while the value of a propensity p designates the strength of a causal tendency for a probabilistic cause to bring about an effect (as events in the world), the value of a degree of a nomic expectability [p] designates the strength of the inferential relationship between one set of sentences and another (those constituting the explanans and the explanandum, respectively). The value of [p] can even be given a truth-frequency interpretation, because it not only designates the logical probability for the truth of the explanandum sentence on a specific occasion but also serves as an estimate of the frequency with which similar explanandum sentences are true relative to the truth of similar explanans [Fetzer (1981), pp. 130–131].

The principle that appears to correspond to the structure of inference to the best explanation we require is the following principle of likelihood:

(PL-1) *Principle of Likelihood*: $L(h/e) = P(e/h)$,

which means that the value of the likelihood L of the hypothesis h, given evidence e, is equal to the value of the probability of e, given h, on the assumption h were true (Fetzer 1981, p. 223). Since this principle governs inferences between sentences, likelihood must be understood as a logical relation (a special case of the notion of degree of evidential support), and the probability involved must be understood as a logical relation as well.

While (PL-1) applies to probability hypotheses in general, we need a more specific version that applies to inferences to laws in relation to the nomic expectability of the given evidence, if those hypotheses were true:

(PL-2)   *Principle of Nomic Likelihood*: $NL(h/e) = NE(e/h)$,

which means that the nomic likelihood NL of hypothesis h, given evidence e, will be equal in value to the nomic expectability NE of e, given h. If we view the *evidence* as the explanandum sentence $Aat'*$ together with the description of initial conditions Rat', then the likelihood of the corresponding probabilistic law, viewed as an *hypothesis*, will be equal to $NE(e/h) = [p]$.

When the propensity for a chance setup (an arrangement or a process) to produce an outcome of kind A on a trial of kind R equals .9 (.8, .7, . . .), then the propensity for chance setups (arrangements or processes) of that kind to produce two outcomes of kind A on two successive trials of kind R equals .81 (.64, .49, . . .). This assumes that these trials were "random" in possessing the same propensities for various outcomes from trial to trial, as must be the case when they satisfy the requirement of maximal specificity. If setups of such a kind have these propensities as permanent properties, their values determine corresponding values of nomic expectabilities $[p]$.

If the evidence consists of two trials of kind R with two successive outcomes of kind A, then the nomic likelihood that they were produced by a chance setup for which the propensity of that outcome = .9 is equal to .81 (for which the propensity of that outcome = .8 is equal to .64, and so forth). Thus, (PL-1) and (PL-2) both support the adoption of Ian Hacking's "law of likelihood," which asserts (i) that evidence e supports hypothesis $h1$ better than hypothesis $h2$ when the likelihood of $h1$, given e, exceeds that of $h2$, given e, and (ii) that evidence e supports $h1$ better than it supports $h2$ if the likelihood ratio of $h1$ to $h2$ exceeds 1 (Hacking 1965, esp. pp. 70–71).

While satisfying these relations would make $h1$ *preferable* to $h2$ as an explanation for the evidence in relation to (PL-2), therefore, that does not mean that such an hypothesis is therefore *acceptable*. That depends upon several factors, including whether or not evidence e represents a suitable number of trials acquired under a wide variety of conditions. However, if m/n Rs have been discovered to be As and repeated trials under different conditions have resisted our best efforts to change it, the inference that the propensity for any R to be $A = m/n$ would then be justified, as we discovered in Chapter Six. For those who would like to pursue these issues in greater detail, a somewhat more technical discussion can be found in Fetzer (1981).

Thus, it would be a mistake to confound relations of preferability with those of acceptability, because even the best supported hypothesis among the available alternatives might still not deserve to be accepted. The inferential situation can be compared to that of a detective investigating a crime. Even though the evidence may strongly point to one suspect among several likely candidates, this does not mean that an arrest is imminent, much less a conviction. The evidential standards that must be satisfied (of probable cause, preponderance of the evidence, and the like) depend upon and vary with the situation, depending upon the type of offense and its seriousness. Scientists can similarly be described as detectives who investigate nature.

DISCOVERY, INFERENCE, AND UNIFICATION

The model of science as resting on inference to the best explanation offers suggestive solutions to three outstanding problems concerning the prospects for a logic of discovery, the nature of inference involving laws, and the conception of science as a process of unification.

These considerations have implications for the possible existence of a "logic of discovery." Hempel (1966), among others, has explained the difference between what is often referred to as the *context of discovery* and the *context of justification*, where the former involves the invention of hypotheses, while the latter concerns their acceptance. While no specific conditions must be satisfied in coming up with an idea (which might occur in a dream, a daydream, etc.), whether or not that idea is worthy of acceptance depends upon meeting suitable standards. Justification thus appears to be the appropriate domain of reason, while discovery appears to be exclusively the domain of imagination. But the situation just may be more complex.

When the principle of corroboration and the law of likelihood are applied to suitable evidence, they enable inferences to be drawn concerning the preferability or the acceptability of alternative hypotheses. But what if the evidence is *not* suitable for that purpose? To simplify, let us say that the evidence is *suitable* only when it reflects stable frequencies within finite sequences in conformity with principles in Chapter Six. If there are no stable short-run frequencies, then inference to the best explanation cannot occur. Unless short-run frequencies for A on trials of kind R exhibit stability, we have no reason to think they are generated by corresponding propensities.

Suppose, for example, that we happen to believe in the existence of the property of general intelligence, as it was discussed in Chapter Three. You may recall that, when two bilateral reduction sentences are conjoined, they have consequences that turn out to be synthetic. Were we to adopt (D4) and (D5), it would follow that anyone who scores between 130 and 200 on an IQ test who works as a cashier always makes correct change. But suppose that we discover that some of those who score between 130 and 200 on IQ tests always make correct change when working as cashiers, while others do not.

Or suppose that everyone who scores between 130 and 200 on IQ tests who works as a cashier makes correct change part of the time and part of the time does not. What would be a rational response? One alternative would be to infer from their scores that they have high IQs and to infer from their failure to always make correct change that they do not have high IQs. But that would generate inconsistent hypotheses. Or another alternative could be to infer that having a high IQ is a probabilistic rather than a deterministic disposition, where the relative frequency for making correct change indicates its strength. That might even be true!

But another would be the inference that perhaps no single property underlies these different kinds of behavior and that a different theory may be required. If no stable short-run frequencies exist in support of belief in a wide variety of different kinds of behavior as different manifestations of a single underlying property, such as intelligence, then we may want to reconsider the existence of such a property. The existence of definitions such as (D4) and (D5) does not guarantee the existence of a corresponding property. The nonexistence of stable short-run frequencies can indicate the absence of a property precisely as the existence of stable short-run frequencies can indicate the presence of that property.

Either way, inference to the best explanation appears to be capable of supporting inferences to the existence of heretofore unknown properties and can thereby serve to define a logic of discovery. Indeed, these reflections suggest an alternative to the inductivist and the deductivist models of scientific inquiry, according to which science is an *abductive structure* that involves several successive steps of Puzzlement, Speculation, Adaptation, and Explanation within the context of the methodology of corroboration and the principles of inference to the best explanation.

Another difficulty that a model of this kind appears to be able to solve has been raised by van Fraassen, who holds that the conception of lawlike sentences as subjunctive conditionals encounters inference problems (van Fraassen 1989, pp. 34–36). Were van Fraassen's argument sound, it would raise an objection to the theory of laws that is developed in this book. His discussion is focused on the following rather general principle of inference:

(SA)   Whatever is A must be B.
        Therefore, if this thing is (were) both A and C, then it is (would be) B.

He suggests that this principle obtains in the case of logical necessities, but appears doubtful for natural necessities. Even though "Whatever is a bachelor must be male" supports "If Jones is both rich and a bachelor, then he is male," other cases that should satisfy (SA) seem to be more problematic.

Van Fraassen thus offers the example that, "If I had struck this match, then it would have lit," does not support, "If I had struck this match and it had been wet at the time, then it would have lit." He credits Robert Stalnaker and David Lewis with the development of formal analyses for such cases that makes them *context-dependent.* He contends that the contextual features that make a difference here are not implied by science itself, which in turn makes laws that do imply them context-dependent, where only *ceteris paribus* clauses might be invoked to fix their truth conditions. (You might notice some striking parallels with the problem of provisoes!)

As van Fraassen must be aware, the possible-world semantics which Stalnaker and Lewis propose are versions of "minimal change" semantics that do not lend themselves to the analysis of scientific laws (Fetzer 1981, p. 35). Indeed, since a lawlike sentence has to satisfy the requirement of maximal specificity or otherwise would not be true, every property whose presence or absence makes a difference to the attribute has to be encompassed by the description of the antecedent of that sentence. The resulting conception, however, is an instance of "maximal change" semantics instead.

Suppose, for example, that the chemical composition, the force of the striking, and the dryness of a match are viewed as causally relevant properties with respect to the outcome of lighting. The conjecture that some such set qualifies as maximally specific in relation to such an outcome can then be subjected to systematic empirical tests by varying the other properties whose presence or absence must be irrelevant if that conjecture is true. When the antecedent of such a generalization is maximally specific, it will be true and remain true no matter what other properties or conditions are present or absent. It will therefore satisfy (SA). The difference between confirmation and corroboration thus appears to be substantial.

The third issue that an abductive model of science promises to clarify concerns the question of whether or not science is a process of theoretical unification. This position has been advanced most forcefully by Michael Friedman (1974), who maintains that reducing the number of regularities that require independent explanation is the driving force behind science: "science increases our understanding of the world by reducing the total number of independent phenomena that we have to accept as ultimate or given" (Friedman 1974, p. 15). In support of this contention, he cites the role of the kinetic theory of gases in subsuming three heretofore independent phenomena—that gases more or less obey Boyle-Charles law, that they obey Graham's law, and that they have specific heat capacities.

From the perspective of inference to the best explanation, Friedman appears to be correct, but not for the reason he suggests. Just as the requirement of maximal specificity asserts that a lawlike sentence cannot be true when it is not maximally specific, the requirement of strict maximal specificity denies that an explanation can be adequate when the antecedent of the laws that occur in its premises include predicates that describe nomically irrelevant properties in relation to the attribute. Even though it may be a law that Morton's finest table salt dissolves in water, it does not mean that that specific law could occur in an adequate explanation.

This implies that theoretical unification occurs whenever diverse phenomena are subsumed as explananda for the same explanans. As properties that were previously believed to be relevant to the occurrence of an attribute are discovered to be irrelevant, the result will tend to be laws of (potentially) broader scope that (ordinarily) reduce the number and variety of independent phenomena in Friedman's sense. The conception of science as aiming at the discovery of laws of nature to secure the benefits of testable explanatory theories thereby promotes unification as well.

The conception of inference to the best explanation supplies the foundation for an abductivist model of science, which appears to improve upon inductivist and deductivist models and to answer significant questions about discovery, inference, and unification.

CHAPTER EIGHT

THE NATURE OF SCIENTIFIC KNOWLEDGE

Recent thinkers have sought to portray philosophy of science as a branch of science itself. Such attempts ignore the descriptive character of science and the normative character of the philosophy of science. Science requires a robust realism for its success.

INSTRUMENTALISM VS. REALISM

Although models of the world can be understood as attempts to describe the world or as instruments for prediction, the realist conception appears to be more adequate than the instrumentalistic. Science needs more than "empirical adequacy" to succeed.

The abductivist conception of scientific inquiry places emphasis upon the phenomenon of intellectual puzzlement as the initial stage of scientific inquiry, where some occurrence attracts the attention of a scientific investigator. Interest in that phenomenon may invite speculation concerning its nature and possible causes, which might be carried to the point of conducting further research, including observations and experiments, in order to acquire additional evidence that might better enable such phenomena to be understood. The evaluation of the evidence by inference to the best explanation could even lead to the tentative and provisional acceptance of a theory as an adaptation to relevant evidence that yields an explanation.

Even though the abductivist conception may seem to be more adequate than any other model of science that we have examined, the argument could be made that other alternatives remain to be considered. Each of the accounts that we have explored, for example, takes for granted that there are observable and nonobservable properties of an external world and that sometimes nonobservable properties should be invoked to explain observable phenomena. According to these accounts, scientific theories not only may but often do postulate the existence of objects and properties that are not accessible to observation. Yet this assumption about reality could be denied, where instrumentalism affords an important alternative to realism we must explore.

Indeed, Popper (1968, pp. 97–119) has gone even further in suggesting that more than one attitude can be adopted concerning the nonobservable. *Essentialism*, for example, holds that science aims at ultimate explanations in terms of essences, where the best theories describe the essences that lie behind appearances. Popper denies that essentialism provides an appropriate foundation for understanding science, however, not because it assumes that things have essences but rather because there is no reason why scientists should assume their existence. Belief in the existence of essences also has the unhappy effect of "preventing fruitful questions from being raised."

Instrumentalism, by contrast, holds that, whether or not essences exist, they lie beyond the possibility of human discovery, which means that science can never provide ultimate explanations for things. Instrumentalism thus abandons the search for explanations altogether, substituting the aim of description and prediction, which might be attained by means of extensional language alone. Scientific theories, from this perspective, are nothing but calculating devices (or "instruments") for predicting future events and thereby contributing to decision making. The world is as it appears to be (through observation), while our theories (about nonobservables) are not.

Realism, by comparison, holds that science aims at true descriptions of the world, which can provide explanations of the phenomena accessible to experience. These descriptions typically assume the form of theories that are expressed by means of predicates that designate nonobservable properties and laws that designate natural necessities. These theories typically explain the familiar by the unfamiliar or the known by the unknown. Although theories are conjectures whose truth cannot be established beyond all doubt, science is capable of discovering previously unsuspected objects and properties, which makes possible genuine forms of scientific progress.

It would be wrong to mistake permanent properties for a variety of *essential properties*, which are properties of individual things "by their nature" that appear in proper definitions of those things. Permanent properties are not definitional but logically contingent properties of things as instances of other kinds defined by reference predicates. Essentialism also imposes boundaries on scientific knowledge, while the requirement of strict maximal specificity, by contrast, insists that adequate explanations explain phenomena exclusively by means of lawfully relevant properties. There are no *a priori* guarantees that explanations we accept today could not be superseded by the discovery of alternative explanations tomorrow.

An interesting conception of instrumentalism has been advanced by van Fraassen, who draws a distinction between what a theory *says* and what we *believe* when we accept that theory. According to this account, to believe a theory is to believe that it is *true*, but to accept a theory involves only believing that it is *empirically adequate*, which means "that the actual phenomena are faithfully represented by the empirical substructures of one of its models" (van Fraassen 1979, p. 158). Similarly, van Fraassen has disparaged the significance of the idea of natural laws by maintaining that the very notion itself appears to be a mistaken one and advancing (a version of) the semantic theory of theories in its place.

Although van Fraassen declines to describe his position as "instrumentalism," "neo-instrumentalism" appears to fit. As Suppe (1989, p. 22) has observed, he attacks realism on the ground that "there are limits to what can be known," where the physical interpretation of theories ought to be restricted to what is observable. His position is also one of "antirealism":

Scientific realism is the position that scientific theory construction aims to give us a literally true story of what the world is like, and that acceptance of a scientific theory involves the belief that it is true. Accordingly, *antirealism* is a position according to which the aim of science can be well served without giving such a literally true story, and acceptance of a theory may properly involve something less (or other) than belief that it is true. (van Fraassen 1980, p. 9; emphasis added)

But surely the plausibility of van Fraassen's proposal to dispense with "literally true" theories depends upon what the aim of science is supposed to be.

The use of language makes a difference here. There is no more truth to "literally true" theories than there is to "true" theories, and van Fraassen is surely not suggesting that the aims of science could be attained by theories that are false. His position thus implies that theories can be said to be true (or false) only with respect to their "empirical substructure." In relation to the standard conception of scientific theories, according to which theories consist of theoretical laws, correspondence rules, and empirical laws, therefore, he is maintaining that only the empirical laws can be properly qualified as true (or false), where the purpose of the theoretical laws and of the correspondence rules is merely to effect connections between observables.

The defense of this conception necessarily presupposes that an appropriate distinction can be drawn between "observational" and "theoretical" language. The fundamental assumption is that "theoretical" predicates do not designate properties of the world. But if observational predicates are "theory-laden," then what is to inhibit the inference that "observational" predicates as well do not designate properties of the world? Moreover, if *theoretical sentences*, which employ a theoretical vocabulary, are neither true nor false, while the observational vocabulary is theoretically contaminated, what is to forestall the conclusion that *observational sentences* are likewise neither true nor false?

Philosophers are masters at the deployment of language to make their positions look persuasive and their opponents look unreasonable. In van Fraassen's case, the redundant use of the word "literally" tends to suggest that "literal truth" requires the satisfaction of a higher standard than that of "truth," which appears to make *true theories* that much more difficult to attain. Moreover, the unqualified depiction of acceptance as involving "the belief that a scientific theory is true" ignores that acceptance in science is always tentative and fallible. *Acceptance* could be described as "the tentative and fallible belief that a scientific theory is true" instead.

At least three elements of van Fraassen's position thus deserve to be scrutinized. The first is that he implicitly defines the aim of science as that of offering predictions and minimizes or ignores the aim of securing adequate explanations. The second is that he takes for granted an observational/theoretical distinction that appears to have been completely undermined by recent research. The third is that he provides a conception of acceptance in science that interprets scientific theories as though they were the final products of a finished process. He thereby distorts scientific inquiry by employing a static model of a process that is in fact dynamic.

NATURALIZED EPISTEMOLOGY

Quine especially has suggested that there is no place for a normative conception of the philosophy of science, which should be replaced by a descriptive conception of philosophy of science as a special branch of science itself. But his reasons for this position are not persuasive.

Quine (1975) has advanced a similar but somewhat more sophisticated form of instrumentalism, according to which, "The utility of science, from a practical point of view, lies in fulfilled expectation: true prediction." In Quine's view, we fashion our expectations on the basis of experience using subjective standards of similarity in discerning resemblance relations between various events. The inferential foundation for shaping expectations is simple induction, envisioned as the expectation that events that have been attended by other events in the past will continue to do so in the future. The similarities between the views of Quine and Hume are striking.

The advance of science depends upon ongoing observation and expectation modification. Science goes beyond simple induction as "a ponderous linguistic structure, fabricated of theoretical terms

linked by fabricated hypotheses, and keyed to observable events here
and there." Like other instrumentalists, Quine retains the
observational/theoretical distinction, while implying that theoretical
language possesses no ontological import. The themes of his essay
are continuous with "Two Dogmas of Empiricism," where he describes the theories of modern science as "on a par" with the myths
of ancient peoples; they are simply better as devices of prediction.

Although he supports the hypothetico-deductive method as deliv-
ering knowledge "hand over fist," the measure of that knowledge is
facilitating successful prediction. There is "vast freedom" in constructing theories on the basis of observations, because even access to
the totality of true observation sentences would not suffice to arbitrate
between the totality of possible theories, which means that theories
are invariably underdetermined by observation. Indeed, he also
wants to claim that there has to be more to theories than their
observational consequences. If there were no meaning but empirical
meaning and theories with the same empirical meaning were the
same theory, there could be no underdetermination of theories.

Precisely what that meaning beyond empirical meaning may come
to, however, is not a matter about which Quine is entirely clear. And
he still maintains that the conception of a single true theory of the
universe is an "illusion" that has been fostered by the success of
science in narrowing the range of acceptable theories on the basis of
accumulated observations. Even more importantly, Quine views epistemology as an enterprise that falls within the domain of science
itself. The theory of knowledge thus becomes a branch of empirical
science, a science of science which cannot lay claim to methods of
inquiry or to forms of knowledge of a distinctive kind.

The naturalization of epistemology appears to generate certain
difficulties of its own. Change in accepted *theories* may lead to
change in the contents of observation. Change in accepted *methods*,
of course, must lead to change in the practice of science. Change in
the *practice* of science in turn must lead to change in naturalized
epistemology. Yet the very possibility of changes of these kinds
should invite consideration of whether the available theories,
methods or practices are the most reliable, the most efficient, or the

most effective to achieve their respective aims, objectives, or goals. Inquiries of this kind, however, reaffirm the primacy of the normative in epistemology and therefore lie beyond the scope of Quinean methodology.

The strongest reasons that Quine can advance on behalf of his position, moreover, are philosophical in their character. As Robert Almeder has observed, there is a certain incoherence in offering philosophical arguments for doubting that philosophy can exist as an activity apart from science (Almeder 1990). Quine's position would make more sense, for example, if analytic sentences were nothing more than special kinds of synthetic sentences and if philosophy could not be properly understood as a normative activity. But we have discovered in Chapter One already that Quine's attack upon the analytic/synthetic distinction and his implied disavowal of explication as the methodology of philosophy are unsuccessful arguments.

Even though these subtle questions of methodology tend to undermine descriptive approaches to normative problems, the most important arguments against instrumentalism seem to emerge from different directions. Evidence that supports belief in the existence of theoretical properties of an external world is evidence that undermines belief in instrumentalism. And there appear to be at least three kinds of evidence that support belief in the existence of theoretical properties of an external world, which result from the coherence of data domains, the creation of technological innovations, and the occurrence of otherwise unexplainable phenomena.

Robert Ackermann introduced the idea of *data domains* as classes of phenomena that are accessible to experience by means of a specific set of instruments (Ackermann 1976). The invention of the telescope (the microscope, the radio telescope, the electron microscope, and so forth) make whole new ranges of phenomena available to experience, where access to further evidence about the world's structure will confirm various hypotheses and disconfirm others, even ones that may have been well-supported by the evidence available by means of previously existing technology. Things that appeared to be solid and impermeable may now be found to have an intricate molecular lattice structure, and so on.

There are several reasons why the discovery of newer data domains makes a difference to the instrumentalism/realism debate. One is that the line between the observable and the nonobservable increasingly becomes arbitrary and capricious. If phenomena that were nonobservable today could be observable tomorrow, then the distinction loses any ontic standing it may have been supposed to possess. The belief that what is being observed by means of an electron microscope is *an intricate molecular lattice structure*, of course, essentially involves theoretical interpretation, but that undermines the very idea of the distinction all the more.

The option remains of denying that the things observed by means of instruments actually possess any of the properties they are thought to possess, as though they were illusions, fantasies, or distortions. If this maneuver was good enough for the bishops of Padua, it might be good enough for instrumentalists today. But as the experiential findings that are acquired by means of instrumentation accumulate and cohere, such a defense appears increasingly less and less appealing. Reliance upon unaided vision may have had to suffice before the invention of the magnifying glass, but the idea that what there is should be confined to what can be seen with the naked eye is nothing more than perceptual chauvinism.

The very existence of *technological innovations* themselves is powerful evidence that we have happened on to persistent and enduring properties of an external world, no matter how nonobservable they might be. The most dramatic evidence has been the development of atomic energy and of nuclear weapons, which have the capacity to release huge amounts of energy from small quantities of matter. Who could possibly doubt that the atomic theory of matter concerns unobservables? Surely, no one who comprehends the awesome power released by atomic fission ought to be inclined to sympathize (even remotely) with the instrumentalist position.

The *predictive success* that attends reliance upon theories couched in the language of nonobservable predicates, no doubt, can be encompassed by the instrumentalist position, according to which theories are devices purposefully designed to relate observables to other observables. So the instrumentalist position remains invulnerable to predictions that relate observables to other observables, when the connections that link those observables were known and even affected that theory's construction. But what of new observables that appear to be novel manifestations of old theoreticals? What about otherwise inexplicable new phenomena?

All kinds of *surprising and unexpected outcomes* reinforce our belief in the existence of nonobservable properties. When a high-flux isotope reactor was employed to irradiate hair and nail samples taken from the cadaver of Zachary Taylor by bombarding them with neutrons to search for distinctive gamma rays that would be released by irradiated arsenic residues had he been the victim of death by poisoning, a substantial set of unobservable properties were in operation. When genetic material is extracted from blood samples of long extinct dinosaurs to obtain minute samples of DNA for analysis by means of polymerase chain reaction (or P.C.R.), the existence of other unobservable properties is being assumed.

Indeed, the potential applications of old theories on the basis of new technologies provide no end of surprising and unexpected consequences, some of which may advance human knowledge, while others might benefit the quality of human life. Admittedly, alternative explanations to the existence of nonobservable properties are always logically possible. But, as Popper in particular has observed, they are not therefore equally reasonable. Postulating the existence of nonobservable properties with endless manifestations thus not only tends to maximize the coherence of our beliefs about the world but also provides a foundation for explaining the occurrence of events in the world that would otherwise be unexplainable.

EVOLUTIONARY EPISTEMOLOGY

Another view asserts that the growth of scientific knowledge should be viewed as an evolutionary phenomenon, but it fails to appreciate differences between genes and culture. When these differences are properly acknowledged, this idea is seen to rest on a faulty analogy.

The field of evolutionary biology investigates the nature of life from its biochemical origins in the amino acids and the nucleotide bases, DNA and RNA, but focuses its attention especially upon the emergence of new forms of life from preexisting forms of life. The mechanisms that are responsible for these developments include genetic mutation, sexual reproduction, genetic drift, natural selection, sexual selection, group selection, and artificial selection, depending on which aspects of evolution are of greatest interest.

The fundamental notion of *natural selection*, which was elaborated by Charles Darwin in great detail, turns out to be simple in conception but profound in implications. Many more members of a species are born than survive to reproduce. This means that the genes of some but not of all of the members of a parent generation survive in the offspring of their offspring. This suggests that those whose genes do survive from one generation to another possess certain properties that are beneficial in the struggle for survival, where such traits tend to make some organisms more fit than others.

The crucial notion is therefore that of *fitness*, where organisms that are more fit are supposed to produce more offspring than those that are less fit. Spelling this out can be troublesome, however, where widespread reliance has been placed upon the conception of evolution as an optimizing process, according to which nature selects those organisms that are best adapted to the environment to survive and reproduce. When repeated through successive generations, this tends to produce organisms that are highly adapted to their environment, as various authors have explained (see Dupre 1987).

From this point of view, it may seem very appealing to suppose that we human beings, as products of an evolutionary process, are highly adapted to our environments, where our mental abilities and scientific procedures are properly viewed as successful adaptations to our evolutionary environment. Indeed, if that were the case, it would be reasonable to imagine that the way we reason and our modes of inquiry are optimal products of an evolutionary process where it makes no sense to even ask if we should reason differently or if our modes of inquiry could be improved. They are open to explanation as effects of evolution, but are not subject to any other form of justification.

Several influential thinkers have subscribed to one or another version of this position, even including (in his later work) Popper himself (Radnitzky and Bartley 1987). Unfortunately, although an evolutionary conception of epistemology would appear to leave no room for traditional epistemology as a normative discipline, there are several reasons to doubt that it could possibly succeed. Some of these arise from the nature of evolution, when it is properly understood, but others emerge from the character of science. They suggest evolutionary epistemology promises more than it can deliver.

The first is that, as G. Parker and J. Maynard Smith (1990) have pointed out, the emergence of optimal adaptations is not easily arranged, requiring infinite populations and infinite time. Moreover, the conditions that are required are seldom if ever realized in the real world, where populations characteristically confront environments that change across time in ways that organisms are rarely able to influence. But this suggests that regarding present adaptations as optimal adaptations requires taking a dynamic and changing process and viewing it as though it were static and complete.

The second, which reinforces the first, is that the assumption that less fit traits will decrease in relative frequency across time confounds something that may be true over the long run with something that is not true over the short run. The phenomena of genetic mutation, of sexual reproduction, and the like, appear to be inherently probabilistic. This means that an adequate conception of fitness ought to be interpreted as a probabilistic property of organisms in relation to their environments. But if this is the case, then the question arises as to the nature of fitness as a probabilistic property, where two familiar choices seem to be available.

On the frequency interpretation of probability, for example, $P(B/A)$ $= p$ if and only if the limiting frequency for B in an infinite sequence of A trials $= p$. The relative frequency for B in finite segments of A trials can arbitrarily vary from p. On the propensity conception, however, matters are even worse, since, as a property of each single trial of the conditions, even infinitely many repetitions of those conditions cannot guarantee that an outcome will occur with a limiting frequency that equals its generating probability. On either interpretation, therefore, no convergence is guaranteed over any finite segment of the world's history, and on the propensity conception, no convergence is guaranteed even over the infinite long run.

Suppose we define "fitness" in terms of probability of reproduction at a level greater than replacement level R within a specific environment E. Then when $P(Ri/Ei \& i = x) > P(Ri/Ei \& i = y)$, by virtue of whatever traits distinguish x from y, x will be more fit than y with respect to R in E. But that does not mean that x will leave more offspring than will y. Over the short run, y may actually leave more offspring than x. And that result is something that neither the frequency nor the propensity interpretations can affect as a manifestation of the meaning of probability relative to finite short runs. Present adaptations might be arbitrarily far from those that are optimal.

Even on the most optimistic interpretation of evolution by natural selection and leaving to one side the influence of "random" or of "accidental" occurrences that bring about changes in the micro- or in the macro-environment, there appears to be no justification for supposing that our powers of reasoning or our methods of inquiry are "optimal" and could not be improved merely because they are products of an evolutionary process. Indeed, the third reason for doubting the tenability of evolutionary epistemology is equally striking, because even if our capacities for thought are manifestations of our genetic heritage, our specific patterns of reasoning and our modes of inquiry seem to be manifestations of our cultural heritage instead.

The difference is one between our *mental capabilities* as a permanent property of the members of a species with specific genetic endowments and our *mental attainments* as transient properties that only arise under specific environmental conditions. Our mental capabilities by themselves do not determine the way we reason or our modes of inquiry, but develop under particular social and physical conditions (Fetzer 1985, pp. 222–225). Moreover, the causal mechanisms that govern cultural evolution—including the language we speak, the methods we employ, and the theories we pursue—are quite different from the causal mechanisms that govern genetic evolution because one is Darwinian, the other Lamarckian.

The difference between Darwinian and Lamarckian evolution concerns the possibility of "the inheritance of acquired characteristics." Acquired characteristics are traits for which we may have a genetic predisposition but which arise from specific histories of learning, training, or conditioning. Fluent speakers of French (well-trained football players, and so on) do not pass those traits to their offspring as a function of their genes. If the children of fluent speakers of French (well-trained football players, and so forth) turn out to be fluent speakers of French (well-trained football players, etc.), then it is because of their specific histories of learning, training, or conditioning, not because their parents acquired those traits.

While genetic evolution precludes the inheritance of acquired characteristics (and is therefore said to be "Darwinian"), cultural evolution permits the inheritance of acquired characteristics (and is therefore said to be "Lamarckian"), insofar as the processes for the transmission of cultural characteristics, unlike those for the transmission of genetic characteristics, tend to be cumulative and progressive. Speakers of French (trained football players, etc.) can teach others to speak French (to play football, etc.) without having to recreate the French language (football as a game, etc.). This is the sense in which, once the wheel has been created, we do not have to recreate it. We can build on what we have already attained.

But, if that is the case, then the very idea of evolutionary epistemology rests upon a faulty analogy. Reasoning by analogy occurs when one thing or kind of thing is compared to another and the inference is drawn that, since the first has properties a, b, c, and d, and the second has properties a, b, and c, perhaps it also has property d. When there are more differences than similarities or few but crucial differences or such arguments are taken to be conclusive, then the argument is faulty and ought to be rejected. To compare the process of evolution to the process of science as if they were controlled by the same principles is a faulty analogy.

Science and technology seem to be cultural phenomena governed by Lamarckian principles rather than genetic phenomena governed by Darwinian principles. Einstein could build on the work of Newton, just as Newton could build on the work of Kepler and Galileo, and progress (in whatever sense "scientific progress" may be possible, a matter that we shall consider in the following section) becomes possible. But if science and its methods are cultural attainments that might possibly be improved, the conception that motivates evolutionary epistemology appears to lack an adequate foundation. Nothing here suggests that traditional conceptions of epistemology as a normative discipline are misconceived.

PARADIGMS, CHANGE, AND TRUTH

Kuhn has appealed to the notion of a paradigm in expressing doubts about the capacity of science to discover the truth about the world. When three distinct senses of "paradigm" are distinguished, the nature of paradigms no longer seems to preclude the pursuit of truth.

Even though these considerations suggest that the philosophy of science may endure as a branch of normative epistemology that explores whether or not various methods of inquiry are effective, efficient, or reliable in relation to their goals, it might still be undermined on other grounds. Ongoing controversies that swirl about the relations between paradigms, changes between paradigms, and the prospects for truth therefore deserve our further consideration. Even though Kuhn does not appear to be an instrumentalist, if his conception of science supports the inference that science is not a search for truth, that paradigms are never true, or that there is no interparadigm truth, the consequences for the account of science presented here could be equally severe. Relativism might simply replace instrumentalism.

That Kuhn has expressed skepticism about truth as an objective of scientific inquiry is not difficult to document. He has implied that scientists do not discover the truth about nature and that they cannot even be said to approach ever closer to the truth: "Unless, as one of my critics suggests, we simply define the approach to truth as the result of what scientists do," he says, "we cannot recognize progress toward that goal" (Kuhn 1970a, p. 20). While conceding that *intratheoretic* uses of the notion of truth seem to him to be "unproblematic," he hesitates to compare various theories "as representations of nature, as statements about 'what is really out there' " (Kuhn 1970b, p. 265). The issues involved here are subtle but profound.

As Margaret Masterman (1970) has observed, Kuhn has used the term "paradigm" in a wide variety of distinct senses. For our purposes, at least three senses appear to be most important, namely: paradigms as *theories*, paradigms as *languages*, and paradigms as *worldviews*. Thus, if it should turn out that truth can be significantly asserted of theories within a language, of theories in different languages, and even of theories reflecting different worldviews, then Kuhn's hesitations would appear to be misplaced. The considerations that follow tend to suggest that Kuhn's concerns have less to do with questions of truth and more to do with matters of meaning.

The conception of paradigms as specific instances of scientific theories, such as classical mechanics when it is defined by the three laws of motion and the law of universal gravitation advanced by Newton, as Kuhn himself concedes, does not appear to be problematic. "Members of a given scientific community will generally agree which consequences of a shared theory sustain the test of experiment and are therefore true, which are false as [that] theory is currently applied, and which are as yet untested" (Kuhn, 1970b, p. 264). Moreover, there would seem to be no reason to think that different versions of classical mechanics would be any less intelligible or any less amenable to experimental investigation than is Newton's version.

A law asserting that the gravitational attraction between two bodies is directly proportional to their masses and inversely proportional to the distance between them (to the square of the distance between them, to the cube of the distance between them, and so forth) would seem to be about equally good candidates for consideration within a scientific community of the kind Kuhn has in mind. What has been implicitly assumed in drawing this comparison, however, are assumptions about shared languages and about shared worldviews that may generate different kinds of difficulties.

Even if truth and falsity can be asserted about alternative theories that are formulated within a common language, suppose instead that they were formulated within two distinct languages. Would this mean that truth and falsity no longer applied to them? Alfred Tarski (1956) provided a partial solution to problems of this kind when he introduced the semantic conception of truth for formalized languages. If we can assume that theories are sets of sentences within a language with a well-defined structure (such as are possessed by the kinds of models **M** of languages **L** that we encountered in Chapter One), then at least a partial answer would appear to be at hand.

Kuhn mentions Tarski and even cites that paradigm of truth on Tarski's account, *"Snow is white" is true if and only if snow is white* (Kuhn 1970b, p. 265). But a more illuminating rendering of Tarski's example, which relates a sentence in one language to its truth conditions in another, might be *"Schnee ist weiss" is true-in-German if and only if snow is white*, a case in which German is the object-language and English is the metalanguage. As long as an adequate translation for each sentence in the object language is available within the metalanguage (so there will be no problems in pairing them up correctly), Tarski's approach would appear to solve this problem.

As I understand Kuhn, however, he doubts whether this presupposition can be satisfied in general. His use of the notion of *incommensurability* as a relation that may obtain between theories conveys the idea that theories may sometimes be incapable of successful translation, where it would not be possible to establish truth conditions for one theory by means of corresponding sentences in another. Indeed, he even appeals to Quine's idea of *indeterminacy of translation*, according to which two theories could have exactly the same empirical implications and yet still be different theories, where translations between them are not possible (Kuhn 1970b, p. 268).

Cases of the kind that appear to matter here involve theories couched in languages whose undefined (or "primitive") predicates have no corresponding terms. Theories that are expressed by means of defined terms, after all, are reducible to theories that are expressed by means of undefined terms simply by replacing their definienda by their definiens over and over until every sentence is expressed by means of primitives. From this perspective, incommensurable theories are those for which the primitives of the languages in which they are expressed lack adequate counterparts. These could not be successfully translated without some loss of meaning.

There is a genuine difficulty here, to which I have elsewhere referred as *the problem of primitives* (Fetzer 1991). Different answers to this problem tend to define different positions in cognitive science.

The hypothesis known as "the language of thought," which is advanced by Jerry Fodor, for example, maintains that every neurologically normal human being is born with an inborn (or "innate") stock of psychological primitives that is the same from person to person and from time to time. If Fodor's theory were true, then "incommensurability" in Kuhn's sense would be an impossibility. There are important reasons to doubt that Fodor is correct, but it should be increasingly evident that the questions involved require empirical answers.

Even though what each of us means by the words we use can never be known with certainty, that does not imply that it cannot be known at all. If Kuhn is contending that meaning analyses and empirical analyses are the results of empirical inquiry and can never be known with certainty, then his position is right but is not at all surprising. This problem is perfectly general and not at all specific to science. Indeed, there are reasons to believe that its consequences should be substantially less significant for scientific contexts than they are for ordinary-language contexts. The language of science relies upon a technical vocabulary of scientific terms with meanings that are acquired through education, training, and supervision.

As Carnap remarked, observational predicates, including "blue," "hard," and "hot," and magnitudes that are easily measured, such as length with a ruler, time with a clock, and frequency of light waves with a spectometer, can be applied with a high degree of *intersubjective reliability* (Carnap, 1966, pp. 225–226). Even when we acknowledge that each of these terms stands for a disposition with various manifestations under various conditions, this only reinforces Popper's conception of *basic statements* as singular sentences concerning the contents of more or less direct experience whose truth or falsity is a matter of decision. For the prospects for intersubjective agreement are certainly greater here than they are elsewhere.

The conception of paradigms as worldviews brings to mind no end of fascinating alternatives. The principal paradigms of ancient people may have been of the world as the art work of a creative artisan, as a living organism, or as dutifully obeying or willfully disobeying a supreme lawgiver. But those conceptions seem to lie beyond the reach of empirical testability. More suitable paradigms of this kind from a scientific point of view, therefore, would appear to be the Aristotelian teleological perspective and the Newtonian mechanistic perspective or, within a mechanistic framework, deterministic outlooks and indeterministic outlooks. Yet discriminating between them seems to be what science is all about.

COULD SOCIOLOGY OF SCIENCE BE(COME) PHILOSOPHY OF SCIENCE?

If the sociology of science could displace the philosophy of science, then matters of methodology might be reducible to surveys of popularity. The values that prevail within scientific communities, however, are not necessarily those of science, when properly conceived.

These considerations suggest that Kuhn's conception of science does not support the inference that science is not a search for truth, that paradigms are never true, or that there are no intertheoretic truths. They do acknowledge the existence of the problem of primitives as a general difficulty that confronts cognitive science, but also as one whose consequences for science would appear to be less grave than for contexts of inquiry that are characterized by less reliance upon intersubjectively reliable modes of discourse. Nothing that we have encountered yet has implied that science is not a rational enterprise or that paradigm changes are decided by a majority vote.

Indeed, Kuhn himself has been adamant in rejecting any conception of science with implications of this kind (Kuhn 1970b, p. 260). He has sought to emphasize the values that prevail within scientific communities and has even gone so far as to suggest that, in proposing standards of broad scope, logical elegance, theoretical fertility, and such, as criteria of theory choice, even philosophers of science have not been entirely mistaken. Moreover,

It is vitally important that scientists be taught to value these characteristics and that they be provided with examples that illustrate them in practice. If they did not hold values like these, their discipline would develop very differently. . . . More important, though scientists share these values and must continue to do so if science is to survive, they do not all apply them in the same way. Simplicity, scope, fruitfulness, and even accuracy can be judged quite differently (which is not to say that they are judged arbitrarily). (Kuhn 1970b, pp. 261–262)

These observations even suggest that research programs in the sense of Lakatos may develop because of differences in the application of these criteria, where different groups using similar rules accept different theories.

Passages like these foster the conception of science as a special kind of intellectual competition, where different groups pursue the same goals by means of the same rules, but where those rules themselves are subject to various interpretations. We have encountered other passages, however, that endorse a less egalitarian and more undemocratic conception of science, where group unanimity is the paramount virtue, "even at the price of subdividing the specialty or excluding a formerly productive member" (Kuhn 1970a, p. 21). And we have also found that science can be defined as what scientists do only by assuming the impossibility of incompetence.

If there can be quack physicians, phony diplomas, and unqualified institutions, surely there can be medical clinics staffed by persons of such a kind. The situation is the same with respect to science in general. There can be incompetent physicists, chemists, and biologists, even among those who possess imposing degrees. So if science consists of a community with the powers of self-regulation, the question arises once more in the following form: are the standards upheld by the members of the scientific community the standards of science, or are the members of the scientific community those who uphold the standards of science? Is there a difference?

A sociological approach to science would study the activities of persons who call themselves "scientists," who have acquired "scientific" credentials, and who are affiliated with "scientific" organizations. Each of them would naturally engage in a variety of activities during the course of their days, including such things as taking showers, having breakfast, reading newspapers, driving to work, reading letters, articles, and books, walking from one room into another, using equipment, writing reports, and preparing presentations. But these activities are also pursued by accountants and bankers, by police officers, and by sales personnel, as well as by doctors, lawyers, and politicians. Which of their activities are the *scientific* ones?

The more subtle cases that drive the point home arise when different members of *widely recognized* scientific communities fall into disagreements with each other. Allegations of misconduct during the history of American science may be few and far between, but a recent case serves to illustrate the issues that are involved here. A paper on immunology that appeared in the journal *Cell* in 1986 suggested that the human body might be induced to enhance its capacity for the production of antibodies that would ward off certain kinds of infections by means of a process involving the introduction of the gene for a protein not naturally found in human beings. Its findings were important theoretically and practically.

The year of its publication, however, a postdoctoral researcher named Margot O'Toole, who was working with Thereza Imanishi-Kari, the senior author of that study, charged that evidence on the basis of which that article had been prepared had been faked. This sensational accusation led others who had signed as coauthors of the report to come to the defense of Imanishi-Kari. One of those was David Baltimore, who was then working in a molecular biology laboratory affiliated with M.I.T. but who would soon become the president of Rockefeller University, one of the most prestigious research institutions in the world. The situation was highly charged.

Baltimore not only defended the report but insinuated that O'Toole was incompetent and had ulterior motives. Since Baltimore had received the Nobel Prize, among his other awards, it was very difficult to believe that O'Toole's charges could possibly be sustained. Nevertheless, when the matter was formally investigated by an impartial panel of experts in immunology, they discovered that the data had been fudged and that O'Toole had been correct. Baltimore offered halfhearted apologies for ever becoming mixed up in the entire matter and publicly praised O'Toole for her steadfastness in the face of adversity. But the whole affair was quite a scandal and received publicity throughout the world (see Hilts 1991a and 1991b).

The case of O'Toole may have been distinctive for the extent to which it reached the public eye, but other cases involving similar principles have also come to light. All too often, the "whistle blowers" have wound up losing their positions and sometimes even sacrificing their entire careers (Weiss 1991). If those who uphold the standards of science not only go unrewarded but are actually punished by other members of the scientific community, while those who violate the standards of science are not only not punished but even rewarded by other members of the scientific community, how can the standards of science possibly be identified with those that are upheld by the members of the scientific community? They need not be the same.

The sociology of science can be pursued only by identifying the target group that it intends to investigate. Without knowing which persons are members of the scientific community, the sociology of science would not know whose behavior it should study. The sociology of science can also be pursued only by identifying the kinds of activities displayed by the members of the scientific community that are really scientific. Without knowing which kinds of behavior are scientific, the sociology of science would not know which behavior it should record. These are reasons to doubt that the sociology of science could possibly succeed without some idea of which persons and which activities qualify as scientific and why.

Both the sociology of science and the philosophy of science appear to stand to benefit from the history of science, which provides a record of those persons and activities that have been viewed as "scientists" and as "scientific" in the past. Thus, the history of science lends its considerable weight to the conception of science as aimed at the discovery of the laws of nature. Given that objective, the philosophy of science attempts to reconstruct those principles and procedures by means of which the pursuit of science might be possible as an activity whose methods are suitable to its goals, since otherwise science cannot properly be viewed as a rational activity. And its findings should benefit the sociology of science in turn.

Indeed, to whatever extent the sociology of science is devoted to the investigation of those features that distinguish "good" science from "bad," the sociology of science can succeed only if its practitioners already have some idea of the standards that define scientific practice. The sociology of science, as should be apparent by now, cannot possibly displace or be(come) the philosophy of science, because descriptive answers cannot resolve normative questions. The standards of science cannot be identified with those that are upheld by members of the scientific community, because the members of the scientific community are those who uphold its standards. Normative issues can only be resolved by normative inquiries.

Neither naturalized epistemology nor evolutionary epistemology nor sociology of science holds any promise for displacing the philosophy of science, which attempts to build a model of science that clarifies and illuminates the distinctive aspects of scientific inquiries.

AN OVERVIEW

During the course of this investigation, we have discovered three (or even four, if the personalist approach were included) alternative models of scientific inquiry. These conceptions differ in their view of the stages of scientific inquiries and of those rules fundamental to inquiry, namely: the straight rule, *modus tollens*, and the inference to the best explanation. And we have explored their respective virtues as conceptions of science. By way of summary, therefore, their essential elements are the following:

Inductivism	*Deductivism*	*Abductivism*
Observation	Conjecture	Puzzlement
Classification	Derivation	Speculation
Generalization	Experimentation	Adaptation
Prediction	Elimination	Explanation

Figure 10. Three Models of Scientific Inquiry

Though the *inductivist conception* appears to be appropriate for ascertaining relative frequencies, it does not satisfy the conditions required for the discovery of natural laws. It follows that the results of its application may be suitable for the purposes of prediction but not for those of explanation. While the *deductivist conception* begins with conjectures about laws and theories that might satisfy the purpose of explanation as well as that of prediction, the results of its application only provide for the rejection of laws and theories and not for their acceptance. The *abductivist conception*, by comparison, provides for the acceptance of laws and theories as well as for their rejection. It thus appears to afford the most adequate conception.

Indeed, if science aims at hypotheses and theories of broad scope and explanatory power (provided by universal and by probabilistic laws) rather than mere descriptive summaries of the world's history (provided by constant conjunctions and relative frequencies) and if the development of hypotheses and theories of broad scope and explanatory power is promoted by the use of theoretical language (with conditional deductive observational implications) rather than by the use of observational language (with no analogous conditional theoretical implications), then the fundamental benefit of the abductivist model of scientific inquiry is that it provides a paradigm of remarkable heuristic fertility for the whole of empirical science.

The general conception that has emerged from these reflections is still very much in the spirit of the Popperian conception of conjectures and (attempted) refutations. These considerations suggest that Kuhn's conception of a scientific community ought to be reconciled with Popper's conception of scientific method by making Popperian training a condition for membership within a Kuhnian community. More generally, the conception of any discipline as a community of practitioners can be reconciled with the normative standards suitable to that discipline by insisting that the members of such a discipline are those whose own practice implements those standards.

The differences between Popperian principle and Kuhnian practice, I believe, can largely but not entirely be accounted for on the basis of two kinds of considerations. The first concern differences between the various kinds of payoffs that normal science and revolutionary science provide, which we have examined in Chapter Seven. Some scientists are optimists and want to try to make a maximal contribution to the growth of knowledge, even though in doing so they run the risk of failure. Other scientists are less optimistic and want to have some guarantee that their efforts will produce contributions to the growth of knowledge that, if not revolutionary, are not next to nothing.

The second have to do with more global aspects of human psychology in the form of the psychological satisfaction and other benefits that scientific theories tend to provide. We would expect the accumulation of anomalies to lead to the rejection of a well-established theory only if an appropriate alternative were in waiting. A well-established theory, even one that is being undermined by phenomena that it cannot accommodate, continues to provide (a certain degree of) *psychological satisfaction* relative to phenomena that it can explain and also continues to supply (a certain degree of) *predictive guidance* relative to phenomena that it can predict. These benefits tend to make revolutions in science rather conservative in kind.

Indeed, the two most important factors that affect the growth of scientific knowledge appear to be *technological innovations*, on the one hand, and *theoretical speculations*, on the other. Inductive and deductive reasoning are evidence-dependent, where the most important sources of information about the world are observation and experiment. But what observations are possible and which experiments can be conducted depend upon the data domains accessible to present technology. Induction and deduction are also hypothesis-dependent, where the most important sources of new hypotheses and theories result from the exercise of the creative powers of the human mind. Variables of these kinds are unpredictable.

Charles S. Peirce (1896) understood this rather well. He affirmed the robust realism that appears to typify scientists and their attitude toward theories. "The scientific imagination dreams of explanations and laws," he observed, where those who would become scientists should burn with the passion to learn merely to understand the natural world. While scientists are among the best of society in their manners and morals, he thinks too much morality can breed too much conservatism, because "morality is essentially conservative." Success in science requires the capacity for imagination and conjecture in contravening and contradicting accepted thought.

True science, he claims, is "the study of useless things," whose objective is compromised when placed in the service of practical ends. Science can only rest upon experience, which can never yield certainty or infallibility. Yet "it is precisely with universality and necessity, that is, with Law, that science concerns itself." While science can progress from an accumulation of minor modifications across long intervals of time, the way science progresses is mainly by great leaps over brief intervals of time. These may be inspired by new observations or by novel reasoning, which can draw attention to previously unperceived relationships within the phenomena.

Peirce observed that scientific minds should not be supposed to be filled with propositions that are certain or even extremely probable, because "[a] hypothesis is something which looks as if it might be true . . . The best hypothesis, in the sense of the one most recommending itself to the inquirer, is the one which can be the most readily refuted if it is false." Indeed, the most important maxim of science is: *Do not block the way of inquiry*! Do not make absolute assertions. Do not maintain that anything can never be known. Do not think we have discovered the ultimate and inexplicable. Do not imagine any theory has received its final and complete formulation.

Peirce endorsed a pragmatic conception of truth according to which the true is that opinion that is fated to be agreed upon by the community of inquirers over the long run. Yet even if we could possess a complete description of the history of the world, we might still not know all the world's laws. Some laws, for example, might remain counterfactual and thus have no instances. Some regularities might be merely accidental and, therefore, display no specific laws. Some frequencies might deviate from their generating probabilities "by chance." Surely this implies that the uncertainty of scientific knowledge is an inescapable effect of the nature of natural laws.

Kuhn is certainly right to the extent to which he maintains that we cannot recognize steady progress toward discovering truths about nature, but it would be wrong to conclude either that science does not progress or that we cannot recognize it when it occurs. The role of technological innovations in granting access to new domains of data and the role of theoretical speculations in generating new hypotheses and theories make scientific progress intermittent and discontinuous. Yet innovations within science and without remain reliable indicators that science has discovered lawful properties of the world. Jet propulsion, color television, and polio vaccines attest to that.

To whatever extent Popper has ever implied that science can properly be understood as making steady progress toward the truth, his conception cannot be sustained. But surely the method of conjectures and refutations does not depend upon any such assumption. The progress of science must be somewhat erratic, including false starts and disappointed expectations. And Popper has provided the most striking metaphor of science as a "bold structure" that rises above a swamp of experience and is connected to the world by piles driven to various depths. We drive them until we are satisfied that they are firm enough for now. Thus, the edifice of knowledge has no secure foundations, yet remains supported (Popper 1965, p. 111).

Peirce was no doubt correct in viewing science as the study of useless things. Pure science has to be pursued without any concern for potential applications, not because they do not exist but because they are so many. The outcomes of scientific inquiries have implications for prediction and for decision and not merely for explanation. When pure science succeeds, applied science cannot be far behind. The useless knowledge of today may provide the foundation for the innovations of tomorrow. But they are not the same thing. Thus, from this perspective, scientific knowledge, like the world around us, appears to be finite, but also unbounded and expanding.

FOR FURTHER READING

Foundations of Philosophy of Science: Recent Developments (Paragon) has been edited to correspond directly to the sections of this book. Many of the most important papers discussed here may be found in that anthology. Any student of the history and philosophy of science should be equipped with a good history of philosophy. One work that I have found to be a reliable guide is F. Thilly and L. Wood, *A History of Philosophy* (New York: Holt, Rinehart, and Winston, 1957). Every student of the philosophy of science should also acquire some background regarding logical positivism. The best place to begin, I believe, is with a fascinating book by A. J. Ayer, *Language, Truth and Logic* (New York: Dover Publications, Inc., 1946).

1. WHAT IS SCIENCE?

Milton Munitz, ed., *Theories of the Universe: From Babylonian Myth to Modern Science*. New York: The Free Press, 1957. A wonderful collection of ancient and modern theories of the universe.

Thomas S. Kuhn, *The Copernican Revolution: Planetary Astronomy in the Development of Western Thought*. Cambridge, MA: Harvard University Press, 1957. A fine study in the history of science from the ancients to Copernicus.

I. B. Cohen, *The Birth of a New Physics*. New York: W. W. Norton, 1960. Revised and updated, 1985. From Aristotle through Kepler, Galileo, and the Newtonian synthesis.

2. LAWS AND LAWLIKENESS.

Nelson Goodman, *Fact, Fiction, and Forecast*, 4th ed. Cambridge, MA: Harvard University Press, 1983. This work has been among the most influential in philosophy of science.

Karl R. Popper, *The Logic of Scientific Discovery*. New York: Harper & Row, 1965. A classic study with special emphasis on testing probability hypotheses.

James H. Fetzer, *Scientific Knowledge*. Dordrecht, The Netherlands: D. Reidel, 1981. Places ontology before epistemology in understanding science and laws.

3. THE STRUCTURE OF SCIENTIFIC THEORIES.

Fred Suppe, ed., *The Structure of Scientific Theories*, 2nd ed. Urbana, IL: University of Illinois Press, 1977. Everything you could ever want to know about theories about theories.

Richard B. Braithwaite, *Scientific Explanation*. Cambridge, UK: Cambridge University Press, 1953. A highly rigorous study of the standard conception of scientific theories.

Fred Suppe, *The Semantic Conception of Theories and Scientific Realism*. Urbana, IL: University of Illinois Press, 1989. Explores relations between theories of theories and realism in science.

4. EXPLANATION AND PREDICTION.

Carl G. Hempel, *Aspects of Scientific Explanation*. New York: The Free Press, 1965. The most influential work by the most influential student of explanation.

Philip Kitcher and Wesley C. Salmon, eds., *Scientific Explanation*. Minneapolis, MN: University of Minnesota Press, 1989. Fascinating studies of past and present approaches toward explanation.

Wesley C. Salmon, *Scientific Explanation and the Causal Structure of the World*. Princeton, NJ: Princeton University Press, 1984. The author of the S-R model shifts strongly in favor of the C-R model.

5. PROBABILITY AND INFERENCE.

Brian Skyrms, *Choice & Chance: An Introduction to Inductive Logic*, 3rd ed. Belmont, CA: Wadsworth Publishing Company, 1986. A very lucid introduction to basic concepts of probability and induction.

James H. Fetzer, ed., *Probability and Causality*. Dordrecht, The Netherlands: Kluwer Academic Publishers, 1988. A representative sampling of recent work on these difficult problems.

Henry E. Kyburg and Howard Smokler, eds., *Studies in Subjective Probability*. Huntington, NY: Krieger, 1980. A valuable collection of classic essays in subjective probability theory.

6. THE PROBLEM OF INDUCTION.

Wesley C. Salmon, *The Foundations of Scientific Inference*. Pittsburgh, PA: University of Pittsburgh Press, 1965. A fine introduction with special emphasis on the problem of induction.

Hans Reichenbach, *Experience and Prediction*. Chicago: University of Chicago Press, 1938. A brilliant presentation of the world view of a Humean frequentist.

Karl R. Popper, *Conjectures and Refutations*. New York: Harper & Row, 1968. Classic essays by one of the most influential philosophers of science.

7. THE GROWTH OF SCIENTIFIC KNOWLEDGE.

Alan F. Chalmers, *What is this thing called Science?* Atlantic Highlands, NJ: The Humanities Press, 1976. A lucid introduction to alternative theories about the nature of science.

Thomas S. Kuhn, *The Structure of Scientific Revolutions*. Chicago: University of Chicago Press, 1964. This book created a revolution in the history and philosophy of science.

I. Lakatos and A. Musgrave, eds., *Criticism and the Growth of Knowledge*. Cambridge, UK: Cambridge University Press, 1971. An invaluable collection of brilliant studies on scientific methodologies.

8. THE NATURE OF SCIENTIFIC KNOWLEDGE.

Hilary Kornblith, ed., *Naturalizing Epistemology*. Cambridge, MA: MIT Press, 1985. Diverse perspectives on the relations between science and philosophy.

Jarrett Leplin, ed., *Scientific Realism*. Berkeley, CA: University of California Press, 1984. A representative sampling of current approaches to scientific realism.

Harold Morick, ed., *Challenges to Empiricism*. Belmont, CA: Wadsworth Publishing Company, 1972. A wide variety of fascinating alternatives to classic forms of empiricism.

REFERENCES

Ackermann, R. (1976), *The Philosophy of Karl Popper*. Amherst, MA: University of Massachusetts Press, 1976.

Almeder, R. (1990), "On Naturalizing Epistemology," *American Philosophical Quarterly* 27 (1990), pp. 263–279.

Ayer, A. J. (1946), *Language, Truth and Logic*. New York: Dover Publications, 1946.

Bacchus, F., H. E. Kyburg and M. Thalos (1990), "Against Conditionalization." *Synthese* **85** (1990), pp. 475–506.

Carnap, R. (1936–37), "Testability and Meaning," *Philosophy of Science* **3** (1936), pp. 419–471; and *Philosophy of Science* **4** (1937), pp. 1–40.

————. (1939), *Foundations of Logic and Mathematics*. Chicago: University of Chicago Press, 1939.

————. (1950), *Logical Foundations of Probability*. Chicago: University of Chicago Press, 1950. 2nd edition, 1962.

————. (1963), "Replies and Systematic Expositions," in P. A. Schilpp, ed., *The Philosophy of Rudolf Carnap*. La Salle, IL: Open Court, 1963, pp. 859–1013.

————. (1966), *The Philosophy of Science*. New York: Basic Books, 1966.

Chalmers, A. F. (1976), *What is this thing called Science?* Atlantic Highlands, NJ: The Humanities Press, 1976.

Clifford, W. K. (1879), "The Ethics of Belief," in W. K. Clifford, *Lectures and Essays*, Vol. II. London: Macmillan and Sons, 1879, pp. 177–211.

Cohen, I. B. (1960), *The Birth of a New Physics*. New York: W. W. Norton, 1960. Revised and updated, 1985.

Duhem, P. (1906), *La Theorie Physique. Son Objet et Sa Structure*. Paris: Chevalier et Riviere (1906). Translated by P. P. Weiner as *The Aim and Structure of Physical Theory*. Princeton, NJ: Princeton University, 1954.

Dupre, J. ed. (1987), *The Latest on the Best: Essays on Evolution and Optimality*. Cambridge, MA: The MIT/Bradford Press, 1987.

Eells, E. (1982), *Rational Decision and Causality*. New York: Cambridge University Press, 1982.

————. (1993), "Probability, Inference, and Decision," in J. Fetzer, ed., *Foundations of Philosophy of Science: Recent Developments*. New York: Paragon House, 1993.

Feigl, H. (1963), "De Principiis Non Disputandum . . . ?", in M. Black, ed., *Philosophical Analysis*. Englewood Cliffs, NJ: Prentice-Hall, 1963, pp. 113–147.

Fetzer, J. H. (1971), "Dispositional Probabilities," in R. Cohen and R. Buck, eds., *PSA 1970*. Dordrecht, Holland: D. Reidel, 1971, pp. 473–482.

————. (1974), "A Single Case Propensity Theory of Explanation," *Synthese* **28** (1974), pp. 171–198.

————. (1979), "Discussion Review: Chalmers' *What is this thing called Science?*," *Erkenntnis* **14** (1979), pp. 393–404.

————. (1981), *Scientific Knowledge*. Dordrecht, The Netherlands: D. Reidel, 1981.

————. (1983), "Probability and Objectivity in Deterministic and Indeterministic Situations," *Synthese* **57** (1983), pp. 367–386.

————. (1985), "Science and Sociobiology," in J. Fetzer, ed., *Sociobiology and Epistemology*. Dordrecht, The Netherlands: D. Reidel, 1985, pp. 217–246.

————. (1988), "Probabilistic Metaphysics," in J. Fetzer, ed., *Probability and Causality*. Dordrecht, The Netherlands: D. Reidel, 1988, pp. 109–132.

————. (1991a), *Philosophy and Cognitive Science*. New York: Paragon House, 1991.

————. (1991b), "Critical Notice; Philip Kitcher and Wesley C. Salmon, eds., *Scientific Explanation*; and Wesley C. Salmon, *Four Decades of Scientific Explanation*," *Philosophy of Science* **58** (1991), pp. 288–306.

————. (1991c), "Are there Laws of Nature? Critical Notice: Bas van Fraassen, *Laws and Symmetry*," *Philosophical Books* **XXXII** (1991), pp. 65–75.

————. (1992), "What's Wrong with Salmon's History: The Third Decade," *Philosophy of Science* **59** (1992), forthcoming.

Friedman, M. (1974), "Explanation and Scientific Understanding," *Journal of Philosophy* **71** (1974), pp. 5–19.

Giere, R. (1979), *Understanding Scientific Reasoning*. New York: Holt, Rinehart, and Winston, 1979.

Goodman, N. (1947), "The Problem of Counterfactual Conditionals," *Journal of Philosophy* **XLIV** (1947), pp. 113–128.

———. (1955), *Fact, Fiction, and Forecast*. Cambridge, MA: Harvard University Press, 1955.

———. (1983), *Fact, Fiction, and Forecast*, 4th ed. Cambridge: Harvard University Press, 1983.

Hacking, I. (1965), *Logic of Statistical Inference*. Cambridge, UK: Cambridge University Press, 1965.

Harman, G. (1970), "Induction," in M. Swain, ed., *Induction, Acceptance, and Rational Belief*. Dordrecht, Holland: D. Reidel, 1970, pp. 83–99.

Hempel, C. G. (1952), *Fundamentals of Concept Formation in Empirical Science*. Chicago: University of Chicago Press, 1952.

———. (1962), "Explanation in Science and in History," in R. G. Colodny, ed., *Frontiers of Science and Philosophy*. Pittsburgh, PA: University of Pittsburgh Press, 1962, pp. 8–33.

———. (1965), *Aspects of Scientific Explanation*. New York: The Free Press, 1965.

———. (1966), "Recent Problems of Induction," in R. G. Colodny, ed., *Mind and Cosmos*. Pittsburgh, PA: University of Pittsburgh Press, 1966, pp. 112–134.

———. (1968), "Lawlikeness and Maximal Specificity in Probabilistic Explanation," *Philosophy of Science* **35** (1968), pp. 116–133.

———. (1970), "On the Standard Conception of Scientific Theories," in M. Radner and S. Winoker, eds., *Minnesota Studies in the Philosophy of Science*, Vol. IV. Minneapolis, MN: University of Minnesota Press, 1970, pp. 142–163.

———. (1977), "Dispositional Explanation," in R. Tuomela, ed., *Dispositions*. Dordrecht, Holland: D. Reidel, 1977, pp. 137–146.

———. (1988), "Provisoes: A Problem Concerning the Inferential Function of Scientific Theories," *Erkenntnis* **28** (1988), pp. 147–164.

Hempel, C. G. and P. Oppenheim (1945), "Studies in the Logic of Confirmation," *Mind* **54** (1945), pp. 1–26 and 97–124.

———. (1948), "Studies in the Logic of Explanation," *Philosophy of Science* **15** (1948), pp. 135–175.

Hilts, P. J. (1991a), "How Charges of Lab Fraud Grew Into a Cause Celebre," *The New York Times* (March 26, 1991), pp. B5 and B6.

_____. (1991b), "I Am Innocent, Embattled Biologist Says," *The New York Times* (June 4, 1991), pp. B5 and B8.

Humphreys, P. W. (1985), "Why Propensities Cannot Be Probabilities," *Philosophical Review* **94** (1985), pp. 557–70.

Jeffrey, R. (1965), *The Logic of Decision*. New York: McGraw-Hill, 1965.

Kitcher P. and W. C. Salmon, eds. (1989), *Scientific Explanation*. Minneapolis, MN: University of Minnesota Press, 1989.

Kuhn, T. S. (1957), *The Copernican Revolution: Planetary Astronomy in the Development of Western Thought*. Cambridge, MA: Harvard University Press, 1957.

_____. (1962), *The Structure of Scientific Revolutions*. Chicago: University of Chicago Press, 1962.

_____. (1970a), "Logic of Discovery or Psychology of Research?", in I. Lakatos and A. Musgrave, eds., *Criticism and the Growth of Knowledge*. Cambridge, UK: Cambridge University Press, 1970, pp. 1–23.

_____. (1970b), "Reflections on My Critics," in I. Lakatos and A. Musgrave, eds., *Criticism and the Growth of Knowledge*. Cambridge, UK: Cambridge University Press, 1970, pp. 231–278.

Kyburg, H. E. (1970), *Probability and Inductive Logic*. New York: Macmillan, 1970.

_____. (1978), "Subjective Probability: Considerations, Reflections, and Problems," *Journal of Philosophical Logic* **7** (1978), pp. 157–180.

Kyburg, H. E. and H. Smokler, eds. (1980), *Studies in Subjective Probability*. Huntington, NY: Krieger, 1980.

Lakatos, I. (1971), "History of Science and Its Rational Reconstruction," in R. Buck and R. Cohen, eds., *PSA 1970*. Dordrecht, The Netherlands: D. Reidel, 1971, pp. 91–136.

Lewis, D. (1980), "A Subjectivist's Guide to Objective Chance," in R. Jeffrey, ed., *Studies in Inductive Logic and Probability*, Vol. II. Berkeley, CA: University of California Press, 1980, pp. 263–293.

Masterman, M. (1970), "The Nature of a Paradigm," in I. Lakatos and A. Musgrave, eds., *Criticism and the Growth of the Knowledge*. Cambridge, UK: Cambridge University Press, 1970, pp. 59–89.

Michalos, A. (1969), *Principles of Logic*. New York: Prentice-Hall, 1969.

_____. (1973), "Rationality Between the Maximizers and the Satisficers," *Policy Sciences* **4** (1973), pp. 229–244.

Munitz, M., ed. (1957), *Theories of the Universe: From Babylonian Myth to Modern Science*. New York: The Free Press, 1957.

Parker, G. A. and J. Maynard Smith (1990), "Optimality Theory in Evolutionary Biology," *NATURE* **348** (1 November 1990), pp. 27–33.

Peirce, C. S. (1896), "The Scientific Attitude and Fallibilism," in J. Buchler, ed., *Philosophical Writings of Peirce*. London: Routledge and Kegan Paul, 1955, pp. 42–59.

Popper, K. R. (1965), *The Logic of Scientific Discovery*. New York: Harper & Row, 1965.

————. (1968), *Conjectures and Refutations*. New York: Harper & Row, 1968.

————. (1974), "Replies to My Critics," in P. Schilpp, ed. (1974), *The Philosophy of Karl Popper*. La Salle, IL: Open Court Publishing Company, 1974, pp. 961–1197.

Quine, W. V. O. (1953), "Two Dogmas of Empiricism," *From a Logical Point of View*. Cambridge, MA: Harvard University Press, 1953, pp. 20–46.

————. (1975), "The Nature of Natural Knowledge," in S. Guttenplan, ed., *Mind and Language: Wolfson College Lectures 1974*. Oxford, UK: Oxford University Press, 1975, pp. 67–81.

Radnitzky, G. and W. W. Bartley, eds. (1987), *Evolutionary Epistemology, Theory of Rationality, and the Sociology of Knowledge*. La Salle, IL: Open Court Publishing Company, 1987.

Reichenbach, H. (1938), *Experience and Prediction*. Chicago: University of Chicago Press, 1938.

Salmon, M. H. (1989), "Explanation in the Social Sciences," in P. Kitcher and W. C. Salmon, eds. (1989), *Scientific Explanation*. Minneapolis, MN: University of Minnesota Press, 1989, pp. 384–409.

Salmon, W.C. (1965), *The Foundations of Scientific Inference*. Pittsburgh, PA: University of Pittsburgh Press, 1965.

————. (1970), "Statistical Explanation," in R. G. Colodny, ed., *The Nature and Function of Scientific Theories*. Pittsburgh, PA: University of Pittsburgh Press, 1970, pp. 173–231.

————. (1975), "An Encounter with David Hume," in J. Feinberg, ed., *Reason and Responsibility*. Encino, CA: Dickinson Publishing Company, 3rd edition, 1975, pp. 190–208.

————. (1977), "Objectively Homogeneous Reference Classes," *Synthese* **36** (1977), pp. 399–414.

————. (1979), "Why Ask, 'Why?'?", in W. C. Salmon, ed., *Hans Reichenbach: Logical Empiricist*. Dordrecht, The Netherlands: D. Reidel, 1979, pp. 403–425.

————. (1984), *Scientific Explanation and the Causal Structure of the World*. Princeton, NJ: Princeton University Press, 1984.

————. (1988), "Dynamic Rationality: Propensity, Probability, and Credence," in J. Fetzer, ed., *Probability and Causality*. Dordrecht, The Netherlands: D. Reidel, 1988, pp. 3–40.

Simon, H.A. (1957), *Models of Man*. New York, NY: John Wiley & Sons, 1957.

Skyrms, B. (1975), *Choice and Chance*. Encino, CA: Dickinson Publishing Company, 1975.

Suppe, F. (1972), "What's Wrong with the Received View on the Structure of Scientific Theories?", *Philosophy of Science* **39** (1972), pp. 1–19.

————. (1989), *The Semantic Conception of Theories and Scientific Realism*. Urbana, IL: University of Illinois Press, 1989.

Tarski, A. (1956), "The Concept of Truth for Formalized Languages," in A. Tarski, ed., *Logic, Semantics, and Metamathematics*. Oxford, UK: Oxford University Press, 1956, pp. 152–278.

van Fraassen, B. (1979), "Relative Frequencies," in W. C. Salmon, ed., *Hans Reichenbach: Logical Empiricist*. Dordrecht, The Netherlands: D. Reidel, 1979, pp. 129–167.

————. (1980), *The Scientific Image*. Oxford, UK: The Clarendon Press, 1980.

————. (1989), *Laws and Symmetry*. Oxford, UK: The Clarendon Press, 1989.

Weiss, T. (1991), "Too Many Scientists Who 'Blow the Whistle' End Up Losing Their Jobs and Careers." *Chronicle of Higher Education* **XXXVII** (June 26, 1991), p. A36.

White, A. D. (1955), *A History of the Warfare of Science with Theology*. New York: George Braziller, 1955.

INDEX OF NAMES

Ackermann, R., 153, 179
Adler, A., 128
Almeder, R. F., *xvii*, 153, 179
Anaximander, 2–3, 8
Anaximines, 2–3
Aristotle, 2, 26–27, 41–42, 136, 164
Ayer, A. J., 128, 175, 179

Bacchus, F., 111, 179
Baltimore, D., 166
Bartley, W. W., 156, 183
Bayes, T., 104, 111
Bernoulli, J., 130
Beth, E. W., 56
Braithwaite, R. B., 176
Bromberger, S., 86–87

Carnap, R., 13–15, 34, 43–45, 47–50, 53, 66, 72, 76–77, 163, 179
Chalmers, A. F., 133, 138, 177, 179
Clifford, W., 113, 179
Cohen, I. B., 23, 175, 179

Darwin, C., 156, 158–159
Davis, W., *xvii*

Democritus, 8
Duhem, P., 131, 136, 179
Dupre, J., 156, 180

Eells, E., *xvii*, 102, 111, 180
Einstein, A., 2, 4, 113, 159
Euclid, 45

Feigl, H., 108, 180
Fetzer, J. H., 10, 36–37, 39, 73, 76–78, 83–84, 95–96, 101–102, 105, 122–123, 125–126, 129, 131, 134, 140–142, 145, 158, 162, 176–177, 180
Fodor, J., 163
Freud, S., 128
Friedman, M., 146, 180

Galileo, G., 2, 4–5, 136, 159
Giere, R., 56, 181
Ginger, 101
God, 5, 128–129
Goodman, N., 28–36, 38, 41, 51, 55, 71, 121, 176, 181

Hacking, I., 139, 141–142, 181
Harman, G., 140, 181
Hempel, C. G., *ix*, *xvii*, 10–14, 20,
    30, 51, 53, 59–64, 66–72, 76–77,
    81, 85–87, 128, 143, 176, 181
Heninger, S. K., *xvii*
Heraclitus, 6–8
Hilts, P. J., 167, 181
Homer, 20–21
Hume, D., 12–14, 16, 25–27, 30–31,
    41–42, 71, 115, 120, 125–126, 152
Humphreys, P. W., 95, 182

Imanishi-Kari, T., 166

Jeffrey, R., 102, 182

Kepler, J., 2, 133, 159
Kitcher, P., 84, 176, 182
Kornblith, H., 178
Kuhn, T. S., 3, 6, 23, 127, 131–135,
    137–138, 160–165, 170, 172, 175,
    177, 182
Kyburg, H., 97, 111, 177, 179, 182

Lakatos, I., 127, 135, 137–138, 165,
    177, 182
Lamarck, J.-B. de, 158–159
Leplin, J., 178
Lewis, D., 98–100, 145, 182

Marx, K., 128
Masterman, M., 160, 182
Maynard Smith, J., 157, 183
Michalos, A., 102, 105, 182
Morick, H., 178
Munitz, M., 1–2, 4, 175, 182
Musgrave, A., 177

Newton, I., 2, 12, 56, 159, 161,
    164
Neyman, J., 130

O'Toole, M., 166
Oppenheim, P., 64, 85–86, 181

Parker, G., 157, 183
Parmenides, 8
Pearson, E., 130
Peirce, C. S., 171–173, 183
Plato, 2, 133
Popper, K. R., *xvii*, *xviii*, 4, 8, 35–39,
    41, 51–53, 55, 71–73, 119, 122,
    127–134, 137–138, 148, 156, 163,
    170, 172–173, 176–177, 183
Ptolemy, 2
Pythagoras, 2–3

Quine, W.V.O., 16, 19–21, 23, 51, 55,
    152–153, 162, 183

Radnitzky, G., 156, 183
Reichenbach, H., 13, 69, 115, 177,
    183
Russell, B., 113

Salmon, M., 105, 183
Salmon, W. C., *ix*, *xvii*, 32, 67–71,
    75–78, 80–81, 84, 95, 98–101,
    112, 114–116, 118, 121, 176–177,
    182–183
Sartorelli, L. M., *xvii*
Scriven, M., 86–87
Simon, H., 105, 184
Skyrms, B., 31–32, 44, 97, 100, 107,
    177, 184
Smokler, H., 97, 177, 182
Sneed, F., 55
Stalnaker, R., 145
Suppe, F., 48, 52, 55–59, 149, 176,
    184
Suppes, P., 55

Tarski, A., 58, 161–162, 184
Taylor, Z., 155

Thales, 2–3
Thalos, M., 179
Thilly, F., 175

van Fraassen, B., 58, 123–124, 144–145, 149–151, 184

von Mises, R., 69

Weiss, T., 167, 184
White, A. D., 5, 184
Wood, L., 175

INDEX OF SUBJECTS

a posteriori, 14
a priori, 14
(A), Popper's thesis, 37, 42
abductivism, 169
abductivist conception of science, 144, 147, 169–170
abstract calculus, 45
acceptability vs. preferability, 142
accidental generalizations, 25, 28, 40
accidental occurrences, 158
adaptation, 156
additive, 109
agents, 102–105
aim of science, *xiv*, 6, 23, 43, 106–107, 124–125
analogical reasoning, 159
analysis, paradox of, 12
analytic, 14, 16–18
analytic-in-**M**, 16
analytic/synthetic distinction, 16–21, 52–53, 153
analyticity, 19
anomalies, 132, 135
applied science, 173
Aristotle's conception of law, 26, 41–42
artificial language, 14
atomic sentences, 15–16

attempted refutations, 119–120
auxiliary theories, 57, 60
axiom systems, interpreted, 45–46
axiom systems, uninterpreted, 45–46

(B), Popper's thesis, 37, 42
basic statements, 163
Bayes' Rule, 104
Bayes' Theorem, 98
beginning of science, 8
belief, 149
bilateral reduction sentences, 50
birth-control example, 68–69
bleen, 31–32
bold conjectures, 133

(C), Popper's thesis, 37
(C') revision of thesis (C), 37, 42
(CA-1)-(CA-4) conditions of adequacy, 64
(CA-1')-(CA-4') conditions of adequacy, 78
causal conditionals, 75
causal-relevance criterion, 76
causal-relevance model, 75–80
causes vs. reasons, 105
cautious conjectures, 133
ceteris paribus clauses, 136, 145

chance, 89–93
classical particle systems, 56
closed systems, 96
closure, 111
coherence, 111
commensurately universal properties, 26
community decisions, 138
competence, 61
conceptions of explanation:
  causal-relevance, 75–80
  covering-law, 63–67
  statistical-relevance, 67–71
conceptions of laws of nature:
  Aristotelian, 26–27
  Humean, 25–26
  logical empiricist, 27
  Goodmanian, 28–29, 34, 38, 41–42
  Popperian, 35–37
  permanent property, 39–42
conceptions of science:
  abductivist, 144, 147, 169–170
  deductivist, 7–8, 169–170
  inductivist, 7–8, 169–170
conceptions of theories:
  semantic, 55–59
  sets of laws, 57–58
  standard, 43–47, 83
conclusion indicators, 110
conditional probabilities, 92–95
conditional sign, causal, 75
conditional sign, material, 27
conditional sign, subjunctive, 28
conditionality, 23
conditionalization, 100, 111
conditions of adequacy, 64, 78
conditions of certainty, 102
conditions of risk, 102
conditions of uncertainty, 102
conjectures and refutations, 127–131, 173

consistency, 111
constant conjunctions, 26, 97
context of discovery, 143
context of justification, 143
contradictions, 17
correct, 109
correspondence rules, 44
corroboration, 139–140
cosmogonies, 2, 4
cosmologies, 2–4
counterfactual conditionals, 28, 34–35, 37
counterfactual idealizations, 56–57, 59, 72
courses of action, 102–105
covering-law model, 63–67
(CP) conditional probabilities, 93
(CP') conditional probabilities, 94
(CP") conditional probabilities, 95
(CRC-1) causal-relevance criterion, 76
(CRC-2) causal-relevance criterion, 77
credence, 99
cultural evolution, 159

(D), Popper's thesis, 37
(D') revision of thesis (D), 37, 42
(D-N) deductive-nomological explanation, 65
(D-N') simple non-causal explanation, 82
(D1) definition of IQ, 49
(D2) definition of IQ, 50
(D3) definition of IQ, 50
(D4) definition of IQ, 50, 143–144
(D5) definition of IQ, 51, 143–144
(D6) definition of IQ, 54
(D7) definition of IQ, 54
(D8) definition of IQ, 55, 74–75
(D9) definition of IQ, 75
(D10) definition of IQ, 75

Darwinian evolution, 158–159
data domains, 153–154, 172
decision-making policies:
  minimax loss, 103
  maximax gain, 103
  maximizing expected utility, 104
deduction, 108–110
deductive methodology, 129
deductive-nomological (D-N)
  explanation, 64–65, 78
deductivism, 170
deductivist conception of science, 7–8,
  169–170
definiendum, 9
definiens, 9, 19
definitional necessity, sign, 29
definitional relevance, 11
definitions, 9
degenerative research programmes,
  137
degrees of belief, 97–101, 125
degrees of intelligence, 61–62
demarcation, problem of, 127–128
demonstrative, 109
determining expectations, 107, 125
deterministic arrangements, 97
deterministic systems, 96
differences in kind, 23
differences of degree, 23
direct probabilities, 95
discovering frequencies, 107, 125
discovering permanent properties, 107,
  125–126
disposition predicates, 48
dispositional predicates, problem of
  defining, 48
dispositional properties, 71
dispositions, 28, 36, 48, 52, 105
dogma of reductionism, 51–53
(DP-1) minimax loss principle, 103
(DP-2) maximax gain principle, 103

(DP-3) maximizing expected utility,
  104
Duhem thesis, 131, 135–136

empirical adequacy, 149–150
empirical analysis, 11, 20
empirical hypotheses, 56
empirical interpretation, 45
empirical laws, 43–44
empirical probability, 140
empirical science, xiv
empirical testability, 6
empirically testable explanations, 6
enumerative induction, 7
epistemic, 23
epistemic problem, 24
epistemology, 23
errors of Type I, 131
errors of Type II, 131
essential properties, 26,
  148–149
essentialism, 148
ethics of belief, 113
Euclidean geometry, 45–46
evidence, 113
evolution, 155–160
evolutionary epistemology, 155–160
exoneration, 108
expectations, 87–88
expected utility, 104–105
explaining the familiar by means of the
  unfamiliar, 4
explaining the unfamiliar by means of
  the familiar, 4
explanandum, 63
explanans, 63
explanation, 22, 60, 63–84, 170
explanation, models of:
  causal-relevance, 75–80
  covering-law, 63–67
  statistical-relevance, 67–71

explanations as inferences from laws, 81
explanations not always causal, 81
explanations not always formal, 82
explanatory power, 170
explanatory relevance, 70
explication, *xv*, 11, 20
explications of laws of nature:
   Aristotelian, 26–27
   Humean, 25–26
   logical empiricist, 27
   Goodmanian, 28–29, 34, 38, 41–42
   Popperian, 35–37
   permanent property, 39–42
explicative adequacy, 11, 14
extensional logic, 14–15
external history of science, 137–138
external world, 148, 153

first scientific theory, 8
fitness, 156–158
flagpole example, 86–87
formation rules **FR**, 15
frequencies, 72, 98
frequency interpretation, 68, 157
fundamental question about chance, 123–124

games of chance, 89–93
general framework, *xiii*
generalizations, 27
genetic evolution, 159
Goodman's thesis (T1), 29–30, 36
Goodman's thesis (T2), 29–30, 121
(GP-1) general principle, 29
(GP-2) general principle, 38
(GP-3) general principle, 41
grammar **G**, 15
group decisions, 138
grue, 31–32

habits of mind, 30
hage, 61–62
hard core, 137
high probability requirement, 67, 69
history of science, *xiv*, 2, 7
Hume's conception of law, 26, 41–42
hypothetico-deductive method, 44

(I-S) inductive-statistical explanation, 65
(I-S') inductive-statistical explanation, 66
ideal agents, 110–113
implicit definition, 12
incommensurability, 162–163
indeterminacy of translation, 162
indeterministic processes, 6
indeterministic systems, 96
indeterministic arrangements, 97
individual decisions, 138
induction, 108–110
inductive methodology, 129
inductive-statistical (I-S) explanation, 64–67, 78
inductivism, 169
inductivist conception of science, 7–8, 169–170
inference to the best explanation, 139–142, 169
inheritance of acquired characteristics, 158–159
initial conditions, 35, 39
instrumentalism, 148, 151–153
intellectual change, 2
intelligence, 46–47, 49, 61–62
interchangeability, 19
internal history of science, 137–138
interpretations of probability:
   frequency, 68, 157
   logical, 76, 140–142
   personal, 97

propensity, 71–74, 93–95, 157
subjective, 97
intersubjective reliability, 163
inverse probabilities, 95
IQ, 46–47, 49–50, 54, 73–74, 143–144

knowledge context K, 67

Lamarckian evolution, 158–159
language framework, 15
language L, 14
language of thought hypothesis, 163
languages, 161
law of excluded middle, 17
law of likelihood, Hacking's, 141–142
law of non-contradiction, 17
lawlike sentences, 27, 29, 34, 38
laws of coexistence, 95
laws of nature, 6–7, 23, 25, 120–121, 125, 149, 172
laws of nature, theories of:
   Aristotelian, 26–27
   Humean, 25–26
   logical empiricist, 27
   Goodmanian, 28–29, 34, 38, 41–42
   Popperian, 35–37
   permanent property, 39–42
laws of society, 25, 121
likelihoods, 140–142
logical empiricism, 13, 51–53
logical form, 16–18
logical necessities, 37
logical necessity, sign, 29
logical probability, 76, 140–142
logical signs LS, 15
logos, 7
long-run propensities, 73

material conditional sign, 27
material conditionals, 18, 27, 54

matters of fact, 13
maximal change semantics, 145
maximal specificity, requirement of, 60, 66, 76
maximax gain principle, 103
maximax gain strategy, 134
maximize expected utility, 104
maximizing utilities, 111
maxims of science, 172
meaning analysis, 10, 20
meaningfulness, problem of, 127–128
mental attainments, 158
mental capabilities, 158
methodological commitment to extensional logic, 14, 53
methodology, 9
methods, 152
minimal change semantics, 145
minimax loss principle, 103
minimax loss strategy, 134
mixed strategies of inquiry, 133
model M of language L, 14, 20, 162
models of explanation:
   causal-relevance, 75–80
   covering-law, 63–67
   statistical-relevance, 67–71
model of science, $xiv–xv$, 169
models of science:
   abductivist, 144, 147, 169–170
   deductivist, 7–8, 169–170
   inductivist, 7–8, 169–170
model of the world, $xiv–xv$
modes of definition, 9, 12
modus ponens, 10
modus tollens, 8, 169
molecular sentences, 15–16
(MP) modus ponens, 10
(MT) modus tollens, 8
myths, 1–2, 20–22, 152

natural necessities, 35–37
natural selection, 156
naturalized epistemology, 151–155
necessary connections, 25, 114, 125–126
neo-instrumentalism, 149–150
new riddle of induction, 31
nomic expectability, 65–67, 69, 79–80, 87–88, 140
nomic predicability, 87–88
nomic responsibility, 80, 88–89
nominal definition, 10, 20
non-causal explanations, 81–82
non-Euclidean geometry, 95
non-logical signs NLS, 15
non-observational vocabulary, 44
non-scientific theories, 128
normal driving systems, 57
normal science, 132–134
normative epistemology, 153
normative standards, 168

objective Bayesians, 98
objective chances, 100
objective probabilities, 98
objectivity, 6, 27, 32, 138, 163
observational predicates, 48
observational sentences, 150
observational vocabulary, 44
observational/theoretical distinction, 48, 52–53, 148–152, 155, 163, 170
ontic, 23
ontic problem, 24
ontology, 23
optimal adaptations, 157–158
optimizing policies, 105
orthodox statistical hypothesis testing, 130–131
ostensive definition, 10

paradigm, 132–135
paradox of analysis, 12
paresis example, 86–87
payoff matrix, 103
payoffs, 102–105
permanent properties, 39–41, 119
personal probabilities, 97
philosophy of science, xiv, 7, 167–168
physical necessities, 35–37
physical randomness, 77
(PL-1) principle of likelihood, 140
(PL-2) principle of nomic likelihood, 141
Popper's thesis (A), 37, 42
Popper's thesis (B), 37, 42
Popper's thesis (C), 37
Popper's thesis (D), 37
practices, 152
pragmatic conception of truth, 172
pragmatic vindication, 115–117
prediction, 22, 60, 87–88
predictive guidance, 171
predictive success, 154
preferability vs. acceptability, 142
primitive predicates, 162
primitives, 10
principle of additivity, 90–91
principle of empiricism, Popper's, 129–130
principle of multiplication, 91–92
principle of summation, 90–91
Principle Principal, Lewis', 98–100
principles of decision:
    minimax loss, 103
    maximax gain, 103
    maximizing expected utility, 104
probabilistic beliefs, 100–101
probabilistic laws, 65, 72–73
probabilistic reduction sentences, 72
probabilistic strength, 73

probabilistic strength causal
    conditionals, 75
probabilistic strength causal conditional
    sign, 75
probability, interpretations of:
    frequency, 68, 157
    logical, 76, 140–142
    personal, 97
    propensity, 71–74, 93–95, 157
    subjective, 97
problem of demarcation, 127–128
problem of induction, 106–109, 115–
    117, 126
problem of meaningfulness, 127–128
problem of primitives, 162–163
problem solving (Popperian), 132–134
progressive research programmes, 137
prohibitions, 39
prohibitions, 128
projectibility, 30–34
propensities, 72, 98
propensities as interpretations of
    probability, 93–95
propensity interpretation, 71–74, 157
proper, 109
protective belt, 137
provisoes, 59–60, 83–84
psychological satisfaction, 6, 135, 171
pure personalist position, 111–114
pure science, 173
pure vs. applied mathematics, 45–46
puzzle solving (Kuhnian), 132–134
Pythagoreanism, 3

radioactive half-life, 95–96
random occurrences, 158
rational belief, 101
realism, 148
reasons vs. causes, 105
reduction sentences, 49–51
reduction sentences, probabilistic, 72

reference class homogeneity, 67–69
regularities, 32
relations between ideas, 13
relative frequencies, 26, 97, 143–144
relevant evidence, 109
religious beliefs, 5, 128–129
requirement:
    high probability, 67, 69, 88
    maximal specificity, 60, 66, 76–77,
        80, 96, 146
    strict maximal specificity, 77–78,
        80, 146
    total evidence, 34, 66
revolutionary science, 132–134
(RMS) requirement of maximal
    specificity, 60, 66, 76–77, 80, 96,
    146
(RSMS) requirement of strict maximal
    specificity, 77–78, 80, 146
rules of inference:
    (Rule 1) Personal to Frequency, 112
    (Rule 2) Personal to Propensity, 112
    (Rule 3) Frequency to Personal, 117
    (Rule 4) Frequency to Propensity,
        118
    (Rule 5) Higher Induction, 122
    (Rule 6) Corroboration, 122
    (Rule 7) Propensity to Frequency,
        123
    (Rule 8) Propensity to Personal, 123

(SA) strengthening antecedents, 144
satisficing policies, 105
science, xiii–xiv, 167–168, 171
scientific beliefs, 5
scientific communities, 161, 164–168,
    170
scientific knowledge, 172
scientific progress, 172
scientific realism, 149–150
scientific significance, 62

scientific theories, 43
scientific values, 164–168
screening-off principle, 70
semantic conception of theories, 55–59
semantic conception of truth, 58, 161–162
semantic rules, 19
sets of laws conception of theories, 57–58
single-case propensities, 71–73, 93–95, 157
Skyrm's Rule S, 44, 100, 107
sociology of science, 164–168
sound, 109
(SPC) subjective probability criterion, 99
(SRC-1) statistical relevance criterion, 68
(SRC-2) statistical relevance criterion, 70
(ST-1) symmetry sub-thesis, 86
(ST-2) symmetry sub-thesis, 86
stable short-run frequencies, 143–144
stages in the history of science, 2
standard conception of theories, 43–47, 83
standards of science, 167–168
statement functions, 35
states of nature, 102–105
statistical ambiguity of inductive-statistical explanations, 66
statistical laws, 65
statistical relevance, 70
statistical-relevance criterion, 68
statistical-relevance model, 67–71
stories, 3
straight rule, 7, 32, 44, 118, 169
strength of a disposition, 73
strict maximal specificity, requirement of, 77
structural properties, 39

subjective Bayesians, 98
subjective probabilities, 97
subjective-probability criterion, 99
subjectivity, 138
subjunctive conditional sign, 28
subjunctive conditionals, 28, 34–35, 37, 41, 54
surprising outcomes, 155
swamp metaphor, *xviii*, 173
symmetry thesis, 85–89
synonymy, 10, 19
syntactical determinacy, 11
synthetic, 14, 16, 18
synthetic-in-**M**, 16

(T1), Goodman's thesis, 29–30, 36
(T2), Goodman's thesis, 29–30, 121
tautologies, 17
technological innovations, 4, 154, 171
testing statistical hypotheses, 130–131
theoretical definitions, 56
theoretical explanations, 82–83
theoretical laws, 43–44
theoretical predicates, 48
theoretical sentences, 150
theoretical significance, 11
theoretical speculations, 4, 171
theories, *xv*, 2–3, 20–22, 43–47, 55–59, 83, 152–154, 161, 171–173
theories, conceptions of:
   semantic, 55–59
   sets of laws, 57–58
   standard, 43–47, 83
theory square, 23–24, 47
total evidence, requirement of, 34, 66
transformation rules **TR**, 15
transient properties, 39, 119
truth, 16, 57, 149–152, 160–162, 172
truth tables, 17
truth-functional logic, 15

truth-functions, 16
(TT) truth tables, 17

(U-D) universal-deductive explanation, 79
(U-P) universal-probabilistic explanation, 79
(U-P') universal-probabilistic explanation, 88
(U-P") universal-probabilistic explanation, 140
(UG-1) universal generalizations, 27
(UG-2) universal generalizations, 28
(UG-3) universal generalizations, 28
(UG-4) universal generalizations, 29
(UG-5) universal generalizations, 30
(UG-6) universal generalizations, 38
(UG-7) universal generalizations, 41
under a certain description, 64
underdetermination of theories, 152
unexpected outcomes, 155
unification, 146

unilateral reduction sentences, 49
universal properties, 26
universal strength, 73
universal strength causal conditional sign, 75
universal strength causal conditionals, 75
universal-deductive explanations, 79
universal-probabilistic explanations, 79–80
universals, 36, 52
useless things, 171, 173
utility, 104–105

valid, 109
validation, 108
vindication, 108
vitamin C example, 68–69
vocabulary **V**, 15

whistle blowers, 167
worldviews, 161, 163–164